Unshakable

Standing Strong When Things Go Wrong

Nelson Searcy
with Jennifer Dykes Henson

The JOURNEY CHURCH
www.bocajourney.com

Published by The Journey Church
South Florida, Florida, U.S.A.
Printed in the U.S.A.

THE JOURNEY CHURCH is a new church that exists to give the people of
South Florida the best opportunity to become fully developing followers of Jesus.

For more information on The Journey Church,
visit www.BocaJourney.com
or call 561-420-0606.

ISBN: 978-0-578-06651-6

Library of Congress Cataloging-in-Publication Data pending

Rights for publishing this book in other languages are contracted by
The Journey Church. For additional information,
visit www.JourneyBoca.com;
write to The Journey Church,
2901 Clint Moore Rd #316,
Boca Raton, FL 33496;
or send an e-mail to
info@bocajourney.com.

To the current and future members of
The Journey Church
who consistently model unshakable faith!

Contents

Prologue
How to Read *Unshakable*
or
Choose Your Own Ending

Did you ever read "Choose Your Own Ending" books as a kid? I used to love them. What could be better than a book that you could be actively involved in? You could make choices; you could read it the way you wanted to; you could skip whole sections and everything would still make sense. Now, that's reading!

Well, you can interact with the book in your hands in a similar way. Instead of simply reading *Unshakable* straight through, I invite you to *use* it. Read it however you'd like to. Let it fit your needs. After you read the first chapter, feel free to choose your next step, based on the topic that speaks to you. Are you going through a hard time in your marriage? Skip to Chapter 4. Being weighed down by financial worries? Skip to Chapter 3. Wrestling with doubt? Skip to Chapter 6. You get the picture. These pages are ready to take you down the path you choose.

Moving forward, let me encourage you to keep *Unshakable* handy. Even if you aren't currently dealing with some of the specific issues that the book addresses, you will eventually. Your life circumstances will change, your needs will change and, over time, you will relate to certain *Unshakable* topics in a new way.

Chapter 1: Weathering the Storm is the launching pad for every discussion that follows. Make sure you read that chapter first and then move on to the chapters that most resonate with your needs. My prayer is that the truths and principles in the pages ahead will meet you where you are and point you toward hope.

Nelson Searcy

Weathering the Storm

Discovering Unshakable Faith

A man of courage is also full of faith.
—Marcus Tullius Cicero

Anyone who listens to my teaching and follows it is wise,
like a person who builds a house on solid rock. Though
the rain comes in torrents and the floodwaters rise and the
winds beat against that house, it won't collapse because it
is built on bedrock.
—Jesus

In the summer of 1985, my family decided to take a trip to Myrtle Beach, South Carolina. I was 13 years old at the time and thought that camping sounded much more fun than staying in a stuffy hotel, so my parents gave into my pleas to "rough it." They also agreed to let me bring along my best friend, Billy.

As my mom and dad loaded up our little camper with the necessities, Billy and I pulled together the supplies we would need for a week in the wild terrain of a South Carolina campground: music, chips, a couple of books, suntan lotion, soda, baseball gloves and two transistor radios – the essentials. We couldn't wait to get there and have a little independence. If things went well, we were hoping we might even meet a few girls.

Little did we know that as we were making our way toward the beach, pulling the camper behind our old Chevy impala and listening to Don Henley sing about the Boys of Summer, someone – or, I should say, something – else had the same destination in mind: a little storm named Hurricane Bob.

Now, Bob was not the most ferocious hurricane to ever hit the area, but that didn't really matter. Settled into our lot at the campground, we weren't prepared to handle a hurricane of any size. Still, like many people do when they see a storm approaching, we decided that we were going to try to ride the hurricane out. We battened down the hatches. We made sure that everything was secured. We did all we knew to do and then climbed in the camper and waited for the storm to come.

About 1:00 a.m., right on schedule, Bob came rolling through. Mom, Dad, Billy and I huddled together by the camper's one small window and watched the wind whip broken tree limbs and loose lawn chairs through the air. I have to admit, I was trembling. I had never faced a storm like this in my life. All around us, the other campers had their lanterns on, watching the damage unfold. Some were out in the elements trying to hold down their tents and grills. We were all in this together.

As I watched the storm play out before my eyes, though, I noticed something interesting: There were some brick houses on the edge of the campground that didn't look fazed at all. In fact, most of the lights in the houses were off, as if the people inside were sound asleep. Here I was scared for my pubescent life and 100 feet away some other kid was probably in deep REM, unaware of the havoc Bob was wreaking. I was suddenly very jealous of everyone in those brick houses.

Well, long story short, we survived. The next day Billy and I bought T-shirts that said, "I Survived Hurricane Bob." Over the next week, we had a great time camping, fishing, barbequing, body surfing in the ocean and, yep, meeting a few girls. Bob hadn't caused me, Billy or my parents any permanent damage. But I couldn't stop thinking about the contrast between us riding out the storm in our little camper and the unfazed slumberers in those brick houses so close by – especially when I learned later that 18 people died during Hurricane Bob's journey up the coast.

I found myself thinking, "How could this hurricane be so devastating for some people and yet nothing more than a nuisance for others?" Here's the answer that came to me over time: *It is possible to survive a major hurricane unscathed if you have the right grounding.* In fact, as I've matured, I've come to realize the life principle inherent in that lesson:

> *You can survive the storms of life if you have the right foundation.*

A FOUNDATION OF FAITH

What do you have faith in? Whom do you have faith in? Yourself? Your spouse? Your business partners? A religious tradition? Karma? An ephemeral God? The universe? Take a minute to seriously consider this question. What kind of faith foundation do you build your life on? Because, whether you realize it or not, you do build your life on a faith foundation. You believe in something or someone. You place your faith somewhere. When the wind starts whipping outside your window, what keeps you grounded?

Jesus once told a story about two different types of people – one who is constantly shaken by the storms of life and another who is always able to stand strong, no matter the circumstances. Take a look at his words:

> *Anyone who listens to my teaching and follows it is wise,*
> *like a person who builds a house on solid rock. Though*
> *the rain comes in torrents and the floodwaters rise and the*
> *winds beat against that house, it won't collapse because*
> *it is built on bedrock. But anyone who hears my teaching*
> *and doesn't obey it is foolish, like a person who builds*
> *a house on sand. When the rains and floods come and*
> *the winds beat against that house, it will collapse with a*
> *mighty crash.* (Matthew 7:24-27)

When your faith is built on the right foundation, you can face life's problems – from the smallest worries to the biggest tragedies – without being shaken. But if you put your faith in the wrong place, you will be building on a foundation of sand. You will struggle when difficult circumstances come your way and, all too often, collapse completely when the strong storms of life start raging.

We would all like to have unshakable faith in the face of life's hardships because, let's face it, life is full of hardships. On any given day, we have to deal with failures, broken relationships, illnesses, deaths, career setbacks, financial strains and a million other problems that barrage us. As long as we walk the earth, that won't change. We will face storms. What can change is how well we are able to stand against the storms that come our way – that is, how unshakable our faith is.

What is true unshakable faith? Simply put, unshakable faith is the ability to stand strong when things go wrong. With the right foundation – one that's built on God and his son, Jesus – it is possible to remain unshakable no matter what kind of storms you face. In fact, through the Scriptures, God has said that he will give you unshakable faith, as you trust him. Take a look at these four pillars of unshakable faith that God can build into your life when you make him your foundation:

Pillar #1: PEACE
God will give you peace when you are anxious.

In the New Testament, the Apostle Paul writes:

> *Don't worry about anything; instead, pray about*
> *everything. Tell God what you need, and thank him for*
> *all he has done. Then you will experience God's peace,*
> *which exceeds anything we can understand. His peace*
> *will guard your hearts and minds as you live in Christ*
> *Jesus.* (Philippians 4:6-7)

Paul is simply expounding on Jesus' earlier words to a group of frightened disciples: "Peace be with you" (John 20:19). Those four words have the ability to wipe away our worries and anxieties and replace them with assurance, if we lean into them as Paul describes.

The same God who created the galaxies, formed the heavens and the earth and knew us before we were born invites us to rest in his peace. His son, Jesus, who raised the dead, caused blind people to see and overcame the grave is the same one who says to us (and I paraphrase), "Hey, give your problems to me." In Matthew 11:28, he (actually) says, "Come to me, all of you who are weary and carry heavy burdens, and I will give you rest." Given his résumé, I believe he's capable of handling our burdens. But we have to give them over to him. When we do, he promises to replace our anxiety with peace.

Pillar #2: POWER
God will give you power when you are weak.

Have you ever met someone who has it all together? Let me assure you of something you may have suspected: That person doesn't really have it all together. None of us does. There are no perfect people. The people who act like they don't have a problem or a worry in the world are usually just hiding the truth behind a carefully constructed mask. They may impress us, but they don't impress God – he sees the truth. God is drawn instead to people who are willing to admit their weakness and rely on him. Why? Because those are the people he can give his power to. The Bible is filled with example after example of imperfect, ordinary, weak people who God uses to do extraordinary things.

> *The same God who created the galaxies, formed the heavens and the earth and knew us before we were born invites us to rest in his peace.*

When we try to match wits with the storms of life in our own power, we get beaten down pretty quickly. We may call on all of our resources and strength, but in the end, what we have just isn't enough – a reality we can all attest to if we are honest with ourselves. Hiding our failure behind a mask doesn't help. But when we are willing to admit our weakness and acknowledge God's strength, we start finding our footing on solid foundation. God will step in and make his power available to us. As Paul says in Philippians 4:13, "I can do everything through Christ, who gives me strength." Why would we even want to operate in our own limited power when we have access to God's limitless power?

Pillar #3: PROTECTION
God will give you protection when you are afraid.

Fear is perhaps the most common of all human emotions. Every single one of us is afraid of something – sometimes with good reason, sometimes without. What are you afraid of? Is it something you're facing tomorrow? Something next week? Is it a financial problem? A health crisis? A relationship you don't want to lose? Whatever you are afraid of, God is willing and able to stand as your protector in the face of that fear.

Our culture perpetuates a misguided image of God. Too often, he is depicted as a feeble, white-haired old man who would seem to have little control over this spinning mass of earth. Rest assured, that image is completely inaccurate. The Bible paints a different picture. Take a look at this verse:

> *The Lord is my rock, my fortress, and my savior; my God is my rock, in whom I find protection. He is my shield, the power that saves me, and my place of safety.* (Psalm 18:2)

These words were written by a warrior. He faced daily fear and tragedy that you and I can only imagine, or maybe get a glimpse of through Hollywood epics. Yet he understood that God was his protector. In the same way that God protected the warrior, he stands ready to protect you.

Pillar #4: PLAN
God will give you a plan when you are uncertain.

Uncertainty is a telling state of being. When the storms of life create uncertainty, we have a choice: We can either become insecure or we can look to God for direction. What we choose is a good indicator of our foundation. When we are not standing on solid rock, our natural tendency is to face uncertainty with an arrogance that both stems from insecurity and breeds more insecurity. We pull inside ourselves and think, "I can handle this. I'll figure it out. I have the bank account/the education/the title (take your pick). I've got this." The irony is that facing uncertainty with this kind of outlook only brings greater uncertainty. You are simply piling more weight on a faulty foundation.

On the other hand, uncertainty can cause you to look to God. And since he is the one who knows how your story plays out in the end, he's a good one to look to. In Jeremiah 29:11, God tells us in no uncertain terms that he already knows our future:

> *'For I know the plans I have for you,' says the Lord. 'They are plans for good and not for disaster. I will give you a future and a hope.'*

God has the plan for our lives. All we have to do is ask him for it. Here's what James, the half-brother of Jesus and author of the New

Testament book, had to say about tapping into God's plan:

> *If you need wisdom, ask our generous God, and he will*
> *give it to you. He will not rebuke you for asking.*
> (James 1:5)

No matter what is causing uncertainty in your life, God has a plan for you on the other side of it. A major part of that plan is showing you how to stand in the midst of life's future storms with an unshakable faith.

BACK TO BOB

Thanks to Hurricane Bob, I learned a valuable lesson during that summer of 1985. I learned that you can survive the storms of life if you have the right foundation.

Now I know what I didn't know then – that the only foundation able to truly weather life's storms is a foundation of faith built on God and his son, Jesus Christ. If you want to read more about how I discovered this truth for myself, check out the *Conclusion* or visit www.BeUnshakable.com.

When you put your faith in Jesus as the foundation for your life – rather than putting it in family, friends, yourself, your work or anything else – God will give you his peace, his power, his protection and his plan. With those four pillars standing tall upon a base of true faith, you will be unshakable no matter what comes your way. When things go wrong, you won't be anxious. You'll let yourself rely on God's strength. You'll have the confidence and poise to move forward knowing that he is protecting you, and you will

You can survive the storms of life if you have the right foundation.

trust his plan for your future. From such a foundation of faith, you'll be able to sleep soundly through every dark night, no matter how fiercely the winds whip just outside your window.

CHAPTER 2

FAILURE

Facing Life's Failures With Faith

Failure is, in a sense, the highway to success,
inasmuch as every discovery of what is false leads us
to seek earnestly after what is true.
—John Keats

And we know that God causes everything
to work together for the good of those who love God
and are called according to his purpose for them.
—Romans 8:28

Whether you realize it or not, failure has been the pathway to
every success you've ever had. We all learn to excel by moving

through failure. Just think about it: When you were learning to walk, you fell down countless times. The first time you played baseball, you probably whiffed every ball that came toward you. When you started learning to drive, you didn't whip right into your first parallel parking space. Life is a series of failures that shape your ability to succeed.

You can either use failure as an excuse to give up or you can let it grow you up.

The only people who don't fail are the ones who aren't trying anything. If you are engaged in life on this earth, you will face failure every day. But here's the good news: Failure is not the negative entity we've made it out to be. In fact, failure is a great opportunity. When you fail, you have a choice: You can either use that failure as an excuse to give up or you can let it grow you up. If you will choose to use failure as a catalyst for your own growth, every failure you face will help prepare you for what God has planned for your life.

History is full of success-through-failure stories. While he was living, Vincent Van Gogh was a failure as an artist. He only sold one painting in his lifetime, and that was just four months before his death. But despite his failure, he kept pressing on; he kept pursuing his art; and as we all know, he is now one of history's most respected artists. Today, his paintings sell for over $100 million. Good thing he didn't choose to quit when failure loomed around every corner.

Michael Jordan, one of the greatest basketball players to ever play the game, was cut from his high school basketball team. Failure. During his professional career, he missed more than 12,000 shots, lost more than 400 games and flubbed more than 25 last-minute baskets that would have won the battle.[1] Failure. Yet Jordan became a living legend on the basketball court. Good thing he didn't let his failures direct his path. Instead, he understood that failures are the bones on which successes are fleshed out.

Let's see if you can guess who this "failure" is: At age 22, he lost his job; at 23, he was defeated in his run for state legislature; at 24, he failed in a new business venture; at 26, his lifelong sweetheart passed away; at 27, he had a nervous breakdown; at 29 and 34, he was defeated again and again for political office; at 45, he lost his run for the U.S. Senate; at 47, he was defeated in his nomination for vice president; at 49, he was once again defeated in his run for the Senate; but at 51, he became the president of the United States. These failures sum up the early career of one of the greatest presidents to ever live – Abraham Lincoln.

Abraham Lincoln faced more failure before his 40th birthday than many of us will face in a lifetime, but rather than giving up, he allowed these failures to cultivate a strong character within him – a character that was necessary for the tasks he would later confront. Many historians believe that Lincoln was able to do what needed to be done in the Civil War because of the faith he had developed over the course of many years of failure. Because Lincoln viewed his failures in the right light, they paved the way for his ultimate success.

FAILING FORWARD

Learning how to deal with failure correctly positions you for what God has in store for you down the line. One of the best examples of failing forward into ultimate success is the life Peter, one of Jesus' disciples. Peter was a quick-tempered fisherman who had already dedicated his life to his family's fishing business when Jesus said to him, "Come, follow me." Peter instinctively understood that there was something special about this man, so he left his fishing nets behind and began traveling with Jesus. He quickly became one of Jesus' inner circle. Later, Jesus went so far as to call Peter the rock on which he would build his church (Matthew 16:18).

One night, close to the time of Jesus' crucifixion, Jesus and all of his disciples were having dinner together. As they were talking about the Kingdom of God and things to come, Jesus made a prediction. He said that one of those closest to him – one of the very people sting around that dinner table – would betray him. We know in hindsight that the betrayer was Judas Iscariot, but in the moment Peter felt the need to prove that it wouldn't be him by pledging his loyalty to Jesus. He stood up and said (and I paraphrase), "Not me, Lord. It's not going to be me. I will never betray you." And Jesus said to Peter (again paraphrasing), "Peter, don't be so quick to speak. There will come a time when, in my hour of greatest need, you will deny my three times in the same night" (John 13).

Fast-forward a few days... Roman officials arrested Jesus. All of his disciples were terrified. First of all, they knew that Jesus was the Messiah, about to establish the Kingdom of God on earth. This arrest didn't factor into their understanding of his plan. Secondly, since Jesus had been arrested, they reasoned that they were probably next in line. So they scattered – all but Peter. He stayed close to where Jesus was being held because he wanted to see what was happening. John tells us in the 18th chapter of his gospel that while Peter was warming himself by a fire near Jesus' holding place, a young woman looked across the flames and said, "I recognize you! You were one of those guys with Jesus." And Peter said, "Not me!"

Peter went on to deny Jesus two more times that night. As the third denial left his lips, he heard a rooster's crow break the morning and he remembered Jesus' prophecy. Peter had failed. He had, indeed, denied Jesus three times in the same night. Feeling completely worthless, Peter ran as fast as he could back to his family's fishing business.

Some days later, after Jesus' crucifixion and resurrection, Peter had an encounter with Jesus that cast a new light on his failure. Take a look at John 21:1-19:

> *Later, Jesus appeared again to the disciples beside the Sea of Galilee. This is how it happened. Several of the disciples were there – Simon Peter, Thomas (nicknamed the Twin), Nathanael from Cana in Galilee, the sons of Zebedee, and two other disciples.*
>
> *Simon Peter said, 'I'm going fishing.'*
>
> *'We'll come, too,' they all said. So they went out in the boat, but they caught nothing all night.*
>
> *At dawn Jesus was standing on the beach, but the disciples couldn't see who he was. He called out, 'Fellows, have you caught any fish?'*
>
> *'No,' they replied.*
>
> *Then he said, 'Throw out your net on the right-hand side of the boat, and you'll get some!' So they did, and they couldn't haul in the net because there were so many fish in it.*
>
> *Then the disciple Jesus loved said to Peter, 'It's the Lord!' When Simon Peter heard that it was the Lord, he put on his tunic (for he had stripped for work), jumped into the water, and headed to shore. The others stayed with the boat and pulled the loaded net to the shore, for they were only about a hundred yards from shore. When they got there, they found breakfast waiting for them – fish cooking over a charcoal fire, and some bread.*

'Bring some of the fish you've just caught,' Jesus said. So Simon Peter went aboard and dragged the net to the shore. There were 153 large fish, and yet the net hadn't torn.

'Now come and have some breakfast!' Jesus said. None of the disciples dared to ask him, 'Who are you?' They knew it was the Lord. Then Jesus served them the bread and the fish. This was the third time Jesus had appeared to his disciples since he had been raised from the dead.

After breakfast Jesus asked Simon Peter, 'Simon son of John, do you love me more than these?'

'Yes, Lord,' Peter replied, 'you know I love you.'

'Then feed my lambs,' Jesus told him.

Jesus repeated the question: 'Simon son of John, do you love me?'

'Yes, Lord,' Peter said, 'you know I love you.'

'Then take care of my sheep,' Jesus said.

A third time he asked him, 'Simon son of John, do you love me?'

Peter was hurt that Jesus asked the question a third time. He said, 'Lord, you know everything. You know that I love you.'

Jesus said, 'Then feed my sheep. I tell you the truth, when you were young, you were able to do as you liked; you dressed yourself and went wherever you wanted to go. But when you are old, you will stretch out your hands, and others will dress you and take you where you don't want to go.' Jesus said this to let him know by what kind of death he would glorify God. Then Jesus told him, 'Follow me.'

Peter denied Jesus three times, so Jesus restored him by asking him to pledge his devotion three times. Then, in the same way that he first called Peter to be his disciple, Jesus again said to him, "Follow me." After being restored by Jesus in this way, Peter went on to become one of the greatest leaders in the history of the early church. He served as the pastor of Jerusalem's church and started the missionary movement that turned the known world upside down over the next 40 years. Peter found his greatest success in life after his greatest failure. How is that possible? Because Peter did not let his failure keep him from being used by God.

From Peter's story, we can glean four steps to walking through failure with unshakable faith, so that failure can be transformed into the building blocks for ultimate success:

Step #1
Face the emotions associated with your failure.

Strong emotions are tied to our failures. None of us likes to come up short. Peter failed Jesus three times and, as all of us would, had an intense emotional reaction to his failures. After failing Jesus, Peter was in such despair that he threw his hands up and went back to his old way of life.

You can probably relate on some level. When you and I fail at something –whether it's at a job, a relationship or a personal goal that we've set for ourselves – we face a barrage of emotions that make us want to give up altogether. Not to mention, the more closely you identify yourself with the area of your failure, the harder it is to keep moving forward. That's why men have a more difficult time dealing with career failures while women are most devastated by relational failures, in general. Our wiring plays into the way different failures affect us.

The key to facing your setbacks effectively is to remind yourself that you are going to face some strong emotions when failures come. Don't let these emotions take you by surprise. More importantly, don't ignore them. Acknowledge your feelings of fear, anger, blame or shame, and do whatever it takes to work through them. Get to the other side so you can focus on the future. As the Apostle Paul says in Philippians 3:13: "No, dear brothers and sisters, I have not achieved it [in other words, I have failed], but I focus on this one thing: Forgetting the past and looking forward to what lies ahead."

When you fail, make sure you work through the failure and get to the other side by doing these two important things:

1. Surround yourself with strong, godly people who will both encourage you and refuse to let you get stuck in despair.

2. Talk to Jesus about your failure. Admit your disappointment and frustration to him. He will be there to help you get back up and moving in the right direction. Hebrews 4:14-16 reminds us:

> So then, since we have a great High Priest who has entered heaven, Jesus the Son of God, let us hold firmly to what we believe. This High Priest of ours understands our weaknesses, for he faced all of the same testings we do, yet he did not sin. So let us come boldly to the throne of our gracious God. There we will receive his mercy, and we will find grace to help us when we need it most.

Step #2
Allow your failures to draw you closer to God.

Failure doesn't separate you from God. God is not disappointed in you when you fail; he's not pointing an "I told you so" finger in your direction. In fact, quite the opposite is true: When God sees you fail, he wants to use your failure to draw you closer to himself.

Whenever the storms of life come at you – whether it's in the form of failure or another storm you are facing – you can either let those storms push you further from God or you can allow them to pull you closer to him. Going back to Peter's story, notice how his failure initially pushed him further from God. He went back to being a fisherman and threw out the whole idea of God's plan for his life. But Jesus wanted to use Peter's failure for good, so he sought Peter out, which led to a turning point. When Peter recognized that Jesus wasn't disappointed in him, he eagerly ran (well, swam!) back to the relationship and was restored. God wants to use everything we go through in life to draw us closer to him, but ultimately, we have to make the choice.

> God wants to use everything we go through in life to draw us closer to him, but ultimately, we have to make the choice.

Is there a failure in your life that is preventing you from drawing closer to God? Is there a relationship that has ended, a marriage that is on the rocks, a job that you just lost or a career that is not going the way you want it to? Do you struggle with a recurring sin that you can't seem to conquer and that makes you feel like you don't deserve God's love? If you are letting failure push you away from God, you are making the wrong choice. Follow Peter's example: Jump out of the boat and get to God as quickly as you can.

Step #3
Identify and learn from the source of your failure.

If you don't learn from your failure, you waste it. So identify the root cause of your fall and then glean what you can from having that knowledge. For example, pride was one of the major sources of Peter's failure. When Jesus told the disciples that one of them was going to betray him, Peter arrogantly assured Jesus that it wouldn't be him. And yet, we all know the rest of the story. Peter's arrogance led to his downfall, but in due course, he learned humility.

Every failure is an integral part of your growth. Think of failure as a test. When you identify the cause of your failure and learn from it, you pass the test. And by passing, you become stronger, wiser and better able to step into God's plan for your future. As Paul writes in Romans 8:28, "We know that God causes everything to work together for the good of those who love God and are called according to his purpose for them."

Step #4
Listen for and obey God's new plan for your life.

The well-renowned businessman and author Zig Ziglar says, "Failure is a detour, not a dead end." When you give your failure over to God, he will exchange it for a new plan. He will replace your negative emotions with faith. When God is involved, failure is never final. Look at Proverbs 24:16:

> *The godly may trip seven times, but they will get up again.*
> *But one disaster is enough to overthrow the wicked.*

Get back up, hand your disappointment to God and listen for his new plan. Failure should never prevent you from reaching your

God-given potential. (For additional teaching on finding God's plan for your life, go to www.BeUnshakable.com.)

Take a look at how Peter's story ends: As Christianity spread into the Roman Empire, the area became more and more hostile toward Christians. The Roman Emperor Nero actually burned Christians at the stake for their faith. Thousands were crucified. Ultimately, the day came when Peter was arrested for being a Christian leader. Upon his arrest, the Roman officials told Peter that if he would deny Jesus as Lord and claim Caesar, they would let him live out the rest of his natural life. But if he refused, he would be crucified.

Consider the irony. Peter, whose ultimate failure was denying Christ, now had his life on the line. All he had to do was verbally deny Christ one more time – but he refused and, as a result, was sentenced to death on a cross. When the time came for Peter to be crucified, he protested that he was not worthy to die in the same manner as his Lord and asked to be crucified upside down. So that's how Peter's life ended – hanging upside down on a cross, never to have denied Jesus again. He went from fisherman to follower to failure…to martyr. That is the unshakable faith God gives us when we follow his plan despite our failure.

What failure are you facing? If you will hand it over to God and take these four steps, he will use you mightily. One day, your story of perseverance may be the story that will inspire others to press on through failure in search of ultimate success.

CHAPTER 3

FINANCES

Facing Financial Stress With Faith

My problem lies in reconciling
my gross habits with my net income.
—Oscar Wilde

Wherever your treasure is,
there the desires of your heart will also be.
—Jesus

Dream with me for a minute. No matter what financial storm you are facing right now, let yourself imagine a reality where you don't live with constant stress over money; you don't struggle to make ends meet each month; you are completely out of debt; you aren't a slave to consumerism and materialism; you are able to save for the future; you have the desire and ability to be generous with people in need and causes beyond your immediate concern. Sound like a nice way to live? It's possible. In fact, this is the way God wants your financial life to look.

Unfortunately, for most of us, the reality is much different. Why? Because we have grown up with a skewed understanding of money and possessions. Based on misinformation, poor examples and our own desires, we have unconsciously developed a certain paradigm for understanding and managing our income. For the majority of us, that paradigm has gotten us into personal financial trouble. Not to mention, our collective wrong perspectives, as a society, have led us into insurmountable debt, broken apart our families and caused continually high levels of stress and anxiety.

As my friend and financial guru Dave Ramsey says, "We buy things we don't need with money we don't have to impress people we don't even like." Have you ever been there? Money has become a way of keeping score. It's as if we are in competition with each other to see who can get the best stuff, live in the biggest house and wear the most expensive clothes. No matter how much we have, we always seem to need more.

The worst part is that we are usually so rooted in our own understanding of money management (or mismanagement) that we don't even realize what we are doing wrong. Like a fish in water, we can't see the reality of the environment around us. We wonder why we live under the thumb of financial oppression, as we reach for all we can get and hold on tightly in our desperate search for security and status.

OPEN-HANDED LIVING

Have you ever heard about how monkey hunters catch their prey? Long ago, an insightful hunter in India figured out that monkeys are selfish little creatures, so he came up with a way to capture them that takes advantage of their nature.

First, the hunter cuts a small hole in one end of a coconut – a hole just big enough for the monkey to be able to squeeze his hand into – and ties a long cord to the other end. Then, he sprinkles peanuts, banana chunks or some other enticing treat into the hole, places it in the monkey's path and sneaks away holding the other end of the cord, to watch his plan unfold.

Inevitably, an unsuspecting monkey comes along, sniffs out the treat, inspects the "container" and then wriggles his little hand into the hole to grab the treasure. With that, the hunter's job is done. All he has to do is yank his side of the cord and the whole monkey/ coconut kit and caboodle lands at his feet.

But isn't there something missing here? Why wouldn't the monkey just pull his hand out of the coconut and run for his life? Because once a monkey gets his hand on something he wants, he won't let go. And with his fist wrapped around the goods, he can't get his hand back out of the hole. If he would just loosen his grip, he could save himself. But he clings tightfisted to what's "his" and finds himself ensnared – even unto his own demise.

It's easy for us to see how ridiculous the monkey is being. If we were sitting at the edge of the jungle watching this scenario play out, we would be screaming, "Let go! That little fortune isn't worth your life!" And yet, back in our own corner of the world, we are as guilty as the monkey. We hold on too tightly. We want what is "ours," and we want it so badly that we are often blind to the consequences of our grasping.

But is what we have our hand wrapped around even ours? In the New Testament, James tells us:

> *Whatever is good and perfect comes down to us from God*
> *our Father, who created all the lights in the heavens.*
> (James 1:17)

Everything good in our lives comes from God. The Apostle Paul echoes James' words and takes things a little further:

> *Teach those who are rich in this world not to be proud and*
> *not to trust in their money, which is so unreliable. Their*
> *trust should be in God, who richly gives us **all we need for***
> ***our enjoyment**. (1 Timothy 6:17, emphasis added)*

Notice the declaration that God gives us *all we need*. You may have worked hard for the money that has come into your life, but God has given you the breath, health, strength and intelligence to do your job. He has given you every ounce of your ability to earn a living.

Notice also how the verse goes on to mention that God richly gives us all we need *for our enjoyment.* God wants you and me to live a blessed life. He wants us to take pleasure in our days. There is absolutely nothing wrong with enjoying the fruits of our labor. We have a responsibility to provide comfortably for our family and to save for the future. God simply wants us to use our money wisely, so we have the opportunity to live well and do good for others. Paul goes on to say:

> *Tell them to use their money to do good. They should be*
> *rich in good works and generous to those in need, always*

being ready to share with others. By doing this they will be storing up their treasure as a good foundation for the future so that they may experience true life. (1 Timothy 6:18-19)

Financial storms come into our lives when we fail to recognize where our money and possessions come from; when we begin to claim ultimate ownership and hoard the good things in our life for our own pleasure. Here's what Jesus has to say:

*Don't store up treasures here on earth, where moths eat them and rust destroys them, and where thieves break in and steal. Store your treasures in heaven, where moths and rust cannot destroy, and thieves do not break in and steal. **Wherever your treasure is, there the desires of your heart will also be.*** (Matthew 6:19-21, emphasis added)

If our focus is on storing up wealth for ourselves on this earth, we will be acting scarily like our primate friends. We will be trading something that is ultimately of little value (treasures on earth) for something of eternal value (treasures in heaven). And as our hand stays closed over our earthly treasures, that's where our heart will be fully anchored. Where our treasure is, there our heart is also. We all know what accompanies a life where money is the top priority: stress, lack and anxiety. Things we've had too much of already.

UNSHAKABLE FINANCIAL PEACE

Here's some great news: You don't have to be afraid of opening your hand and giving control of your financial life over to God. There is nothing more freeing. When you open your hand and give something that's difficult to deal with over to God, he replaces that empty space in your palm with peace. So as you learn to release control of your money back to God, he will replace the raging storm of financial stress with unshakable financial peace.

The reason so few of us have taken this step toward peace is because 1) we don't realize we need to and 2) we don't know how. Unfortunately, the topic of God-honoring financial management (aka "stewardship") has become taboo. People in positions of Christian leadership have long been afraid to broach the subject, which has left everyone else confused. But stewardship is part of life. We are stewards of our time, our talents...and our money. We'll never be able to live the life God created us to live without first learning how to handle our resources the way God intends.

We'll never be able to live the life God created us to live without first learning how to handle our resources the way God intends.

Jesus was never afraid to talk about money. Outside of the Kingdom of God, stewardship was his favorite subject. He talked more about money and possessions than about faith and prayer combined. In fact, there are 2,350 verses in the Bible that talk about money and how to deal with money. If I were asked to sum up all of his teaching on money and possessions in one sentence, it would be this: *Live an open-handed life.*

If we want God to be able to trust us with his true purposes for us on this earth and true riches in heaven, we must live a life of generosity rather than a life of selfishness and greed. As we do, he will be able to begin blessing and using us beyond belief. In Luke 16:11, Jesus says:

> *If you are untrustworthy about worldly wealth, who will trust you with the true riches of heaven?*

If you are blocking God's blessing by handling your finances incorrectly, you will miss out on privileges that can be considered life's true riches – riches such as making a difference with your life, investing in other people and being able to leave a legacy.

As long as money takes priority over God, you will never be able to become a trustworthy steward. Being trustworthy means understanding that God owns everything, that you are a manager of what he has given you on this earth and that you are called to live an open-handed life of generosity. When you understand the significance of these truths and live accordingly, you can quell the financial storms around you and finally find peace. But to get there, you have to take these four important steps:

1. Determine your priorities.

Whether we are talking about time, relationships or money, stewardship is ultimately about priorities. What you consider to be important determines how you treat the things that have been allocated to you. Consider these two scenarios:

Scenario Number One – A couple in your neighborhood earns a combined income of $120,000 per year. Not too little, by any means, but not extravagant. But there's a little problem – they are spending $130,000 per year.

Scenario Number Two – Another couple in your neighborhood also earns $120,000. This couple only spends $115,000 per year.

The couple in Scenario Two will have much more financial peace than the couple in Scenario One because they spend less money than they make in a given year. Financial Peace has nothing to do with how much you make and everything to do with how much you spend. Or to put it another way, financial peace has nothing to do with how much you make and everything to do with *how you use what you make.*

You may be pulling down more money right now that you ever expected to be earning, yet you probably have more stress than ever before. As your income has increased your financial peace has decreased. Why? Because your priorities are out of line. The difference between the two couples in our scenario boils down to one word: prioritics. Priorities are a major stepping-stone toward financial peace. Right Priorities = Peace.

So you have to ask yourself, "What am I putting first in my financial life?" Are your own desires taking the top position? As part of the greatest message Jesus ever taught, the Sermon on the Mount, he said:

> *Seek first His kingdom and His righteousness, and all*
> *these things will be added to you.* (Matthew 6:33, NASB)

The Message translation (in more context) puts it this way:

> *If God gives such attention to the appearance of*
> *wildflowers – most of which are never even seen – don't*
> *you think he'll attend to you, take pride in you, do his best*
> *for you? What I'm trying to do here is to get you to relax,*
> *to not be so preoccupied with getting, so you can respond*
> *to God's giving. People who don't know God and the way*
> *he works fuss over these things, but you know both God*

and how he works. Steep your life in God-reality, God-initiative, God-provisions. Don't worry about missing out. You'll find all your everyday human concerns will be met.
(Matthew 6:30-33, MSG)

When you make God your top priority, everything else in your life will fall in line. Proper priorities lead to proper living; improper priorities lead to improper living. So, what does it look like to manage money in a way that gives God top priority?

First of all, don't close your fist around your money. Instead, open your hand and say, "God, thank you for giving me this dollar. How do you want me to use it?" Then, using percentages, you start telling that sum of money where to go. (Have you noticed that if you don't tell your money where to go, it will just disappear?) The first 10% of your money goes back to God as a tithe. He gave you the knowledge, strength and ability to earn the money to begin with. Following the command to tithe opens you up to a life full of God's blessing. (Tithing is a big discussion. To study it further, see my book, *The Generosity Ladder* by Nelson Searcy, Baker Books 2010.)

Once you tithe the first 10%, the second 10% goes to pay off debt, and the third 10% goes into savings. If you are out of debt, congratulations! You should put the second 10% into savings and invest the third 10%. The key is to learn to live on 70% of your income. Unfortunately, most people are living on 110% of their income, spending everything they've got and then using credit to spend even more.

You may be thinking, "If I earned more, then maybe I could live on 70%," but that's simply not true. Studies prove that every time our earnings go up, our lifestyles go up accordingly and we continue to live with little to no margin in our financial lives. We have to make a decision to end the cycle. With God's help, you can break the bond of materialism; you can decide to get out of debt; you can start saving for the future. When he is your top priority, you will handle your money differently and you will be blessed more than you can imagine.

The 70% Principle of Lasting Wealth

Imagine a sum of money (like your paycheck!) comes into your life. What do you do? First of all, you don't close your fist around it; you keep your hand open and thank God for it. Then you tell it where to go:

If you are not in debt…

- The first 10% goes to your **tithe.**
- The second 10% goes into **savings.**
- The third 10% goes toward **investments**.

If you are in debt…

- The first 10% goes to your **tithe.**
- The second 10% goes to pay off **debt**.
- The third 10% goes into **savings**.

One of the major keys to reaching financial peace is:
Learn to live on 70% of your income.

For more detailed teaching on this principle or for more info on wise financial planning, see my book The Generosity Ladder *by Nelson Searcy (Baker Books, 2010) and check out www.BeUnshakable.com.*

---

2. Decide to get out of debt.

The average American carries over $17,000 of debt. Are you average? Above average? If you've ever been in a significant amount of debt, you know how the stress of it weighs you down. Millions in this country lie awake at night worried about the money they owe to others, whether those "others" be individuals or credit companies. Many of us have accepted the cultural lie that debt is just a way of life. We think we could never live happily or maintain a good lifestyle without going into debt.

In reality, debt is neither necessary nor admirable. In fact, the Bible says that someone who borrows money becomes slave to the one who lends it (Proverbs 22:7). Have you ever felt like a slave to your credit card company? It also calls those who borrow and don't repay "wicked" (Psalm 37:21). There is a better way to live. God doesn't intend for us to owe anyone anything but love (Romans 13:8).

Getting out of debt is a process that begins with a decision. Making that decision is one of the wisest steps you can take toward financial peace. Once you *decide* that you don't want to live with the stress and anxiety of debt, you can begin the process of becoming debt-free. Not only that, but your decision will please God. You'll be putting yourself in a position where he is better able to bless you.

Understanding *The Principle of Contentment* is key to getting out of debt. *The Principle of Contentment* is a name I've given to discovering how to be content with what you have rather than being obsessed over getting more. Hebrews 13:5 says:

> *Don't love money; be satisfied with what you have. For God*
> *has said, 'I will never fail you. I will never abandon you.'*

When you are operating out of *The Principle of Contentment*, you don't always have to have the latest and greatest toy or fashion. You don't have to run out and buy the newest iPhone; you can be content with the one you are using – the one that was the greatest thing ever last year. You don't have to have those new shoes; you can get one more season out of the ones you already have. By implementing this principle, you can stop going further in debt buying things you don't really need, and you can begin to dig your way out of the debt you've already accumulated. When you are finally debt free, you'll be able to pay for the things you want on the spot, rather than with an interest payment that causes you to end up ultimately dishing out three times the cost of the item. That alone would be a huge step toward financial peace. (For more on getting out of debt and creating a solid financial plan, see *The Total Money Makeover* by Dave Ramsey and www.BeUnshakable.com.)

3. Discipline yourself in small financial ways.

Small, everyday decision can lead to revolutions. You've probably heard the saying, "The devil is in the details." Well, I like to spin that a bit. Actually, God is in the details. The Bible says that if we are faithful with the little things in life, then God will entrust us with more. How we deal with details matters, especially when it comes to money. In fact, Jesus once said (to a group of religious leaders who thought of themselves more highly than they should have):

> *If you are faithful in little things, you will be faithful in large ones. But if you are dishonest in little things, you won't be honest with greater responsibilities. And if you are untrustworthy about worldly wealth, who will trust*

you with the true riches of heaven? And if you are not faithful with other people's things, why should you be trusted with things of your own? No one can serve two masters.... You cannot serve both God and money. (Luke 16:10-13)

We all want to be entrusted with more. That's our nature. We want to be approved of and promoted; we want someone to have faith in our abilities and trust us with added responsibility. But to get to the point where we can be trusted with more, we have to first prove ourselves faithful with what we've already been given. How? By disciplining ourselves in small ways.

Without even thinking, you probably make daily decisions about your finances that could be considered unwise. By simply examining your spending habits and deciding to discipline yourself, you could prove that you are faithful with what you have and ready to handle greater responsibility. Here's an example:

In the area of town where I work, it costs between $12 and $15 to go out to lunch. If I pop out to a restaurant and get a salad or a sandwich and a drink, I can expect to pay a minimum of $12. When I examine this decision, I realize that I would be wise to discipline myself in a small way by bringing my lunch to work at least four out of five days. The sandwich I make myself at home would only cost me about $1, so in essence, I am saving at least $11 per day, four days per week. That's $44 per week, almost $200 per month and around $2,290 per year.

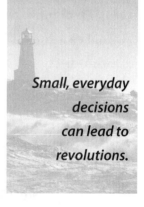

Small, everyday decisions can lead to revolutions.

Just think about that: I am saving close to $3,000, and probably doing my health a favor, by making the small decision to bring my lunch to work four days of the week and only go out one. Over three years, that's $9,000. Knowing that I am saving that kind of money makes my homemade sandwiches taste more delicious than anything I could buy in a restaurant.

A small decision like this can bring a lot of financial peace into your life. If you are in debt, you could use that money to start paying off what you owe. If you need to invest for the future, there's $3,000 you didn't have last year – add it to a money market account and start earning higher dividends. Or you could continue choosing to eat it. It's up to you to decide your level of wisdom and faithfulness in the small things. Just keep Jesus' promise in mind.

If you were to interview the wealthiest people in America, you may be surprised to find that they are the kind of people who eat humble lunches. They often drive slightly older cars. Studies show that the vast majority of wealthy people are not extravagant. Rather, they make small exchanges every day to make sure they stay on the path to wealth.

Disciplining yourself in small financial ways every day ultimately makes a huge difference in your overall financial picture. People who discipline themselves don't run into major financial storms; they have financial peace. In Galatians, Paul gives us a word of encouragement:

> *So let's not get tired of doing what is good. At just the right time we will reap a harvest of blessing if we don't give up.* (Galatians 6:9)

Discipline yourself in small financial ways and you will put yourself in a position for God to bless you with even greater riches.

4. Discover the joy of generosity.

An inclination to give is written on your soul, no matter how diluted it may be. Sometimes it takes a traumatic experience to bring that God-given pull toward generosity to the surface. Horror novelist Stephen King is not someone who is usually associated with biblical principles, but he definitely understands this one. In a commencement speech delivered to Vassar graduates a few years ago, he offered some insight to his audience on living an open-handed life. Here's an excerpt of his comments:

> *A couple of years ago I found out what "you can't take it with you" means. I found out while I was lying in a ditch at the side of a country road, covered with mud and blood and with the tibia of my right leg poking out the side of my jeans like a branch of a tree taken down in a thunderstorm. I had a MasterCard in my wallet, but when you're lying in a ditch with broken glass in your hair, no one accepts MasterCard.*
>
> *We all know that life is ephemeral, but on that particular day and in the months that followed, I got a painful but extremely valuable look at life's simple backstage truths. We come in naked and broke. We may be dressed when we go out, but we're just as broke. Warren Buffett? Going to go out broke. Bill Gates? Going out broke. Tom Hanks? Going out broke. Steve King? Broke. Not a crying dime.*
>
> *All the money you earn, all the stocks you buy, all the mutual funds you trade – all of that is mostly smoke and mirrors. It's still going to be a quarter-past getting late whether you tell the time on a Timex or a Rolex. No matter how large your bank account, no matter how many credit*

cards you have, sooner or later things will begin to go wrong with the only three things you have that you can really call your own: your body, your spirit and your mind.

So I want you to consider making your life one long gift to others. And why not? All you have is on loan, anyway. All that lasts is what you pass on...

... we have the power to help, the power to change. And why should we refuse? Because we're going to take it with us? Please. Giving is a way of taking the focus off the money we make and putting it back where it belongs – on the lives we lead, the families we raise, the communities that nurture us.

A life of giving – not just money, but time and spirit – repays. It helps us remember that we may be going out broke, but right now we're doing OK. Right now we have the power to do great good for others and for ourselves.

So I ask you to begin giving, and to continue as you began. I think you'll find in the end that you got far more than you ever had, and did more good than you ever dreamed.[2]

Who knows how familiar Mr. King is with the Old Testament but, intentionally or otherwise, his remarks perfectly echo the book of Ecclesiastes' observation that:

We all come to the end of our lives as naked and empty-handed as on the day we were born. We can't take our riches with us. (Ecclesiastes 5:15)

They also speak to the mindset that takes the sting out of this condition, per Jesus:

It is more blessed to give than to receive. (Acts 20:35)

You have probably discovered for yourself that there really is more joy in giving than in receiving. Coming to this realization is key to living an open-handed life. We all figure this out sooner or later, if we are honest. Think about your experience around the holidays. When I was a young, I loved to get Christmas presents. But as I got older, the presents became less and less important to me. Now that I have a wife and family of my own, I have discovered that the true joy has nothing to do with getting gifts, but with giving gifts to the people I love. Have you felt that yet? Giving truly is more fun than receiving.

The words "miser" and "miserable" obviously come from the same root word. Misers live a closed-fisted life and end up miserable. On the other hand, generous people experience the joy that comes with open-handed living. One of the reasons it feels so good to give is because when we give, we are actually reflecting the heart of God. God is a giving God. You've probably heard the famous verse from the book of John:

> *For God loved the world so much that he gave his one and*
> *only Son, so that everyone who believes in him will not*
> *perish but have eternal life.* (John 3:16)

God gave us the thing that was most precious to him – his son. When we give, we are acting like God. No wonder there is so much power in generosity. (For more on living a generous life, see *The Generosity Ladder*, Baker Books 2010.)

Let me encourage you to begin taking these four steps toward financial peace today. Think about your priorities, decide to get out of consumer debt, start disciplining yourself in small financial ways and embrace the good that comes with living an open-handed life of generosity. There is always a reason to put decisions like this off until tomorrow (which is why so many of us end up in financial crisis), so I challenge you to begin walking the path toward effective money management today. Whatever financial storms are in your life right now, they will begin to subside as you discover how to trust God with all of your resources – and as you do, he will replace your financial stress with financial peace.

CHAPTER 4

MARRIAGE

Facing Marriage Problems With Faith
or
The Ultimate Marriage Survival Kit

A successful marriage is an edifice
that must be rebuilt every day.
—Andre Maurois

So now I am giving you a new commandment:
Love each other. Just as I have loved you,
you should love each other.
—Jesus

We've all heard the sobering statistics about marriage. The fact that more than half of the marriages in America end in divorce has, sadly, become something of a cultural norm. Too many people today think of the marriage relationship as a temporary contract – something they get into with the best of intentions but without much concern because they know they can get out whenever they want. The very idea of marriage in our society is being called into question daily. Just consider all of the rampant public and political debate over the traditional, biblical understanding of marriage. Is marriage really one man and one woman together forever? Or is it something else? Marriage's true heart is under attack.

Given the hostile climate toward marriage that permeates our society, protecting our marriages is harder – but more important – than ever before. Our marriages are in a war, just as many of us individually are at war within them. In any kind of threatening situation like this, it helps to have a survival kit handy – one filled with the essential tools for staying safe and helping us get back to the place of peace and love that we inhabited when we first took our marriage vows. When we view our marriages through the right lens and put some tools to work to protect our sacred union from the ravages of the world, we can have marriages that not only survive but also actually thrive.

SURVIVING AND THRIVING IN YOUR MARRIAGE

God has a plan for your marriage. He wants it to be a strong, unshakable union of mutual love and respect. Just look at what Jesus has to say about marriage, as recorded by his disciple Matthew:

Some Pharisees came and tried to trap [Jesus] with this question: 'Should a man be allowed to divorce his wife for just any reason?'

'Haven't you read the Scriptures?' Jesus replied. 'They record that from the beginning God made them male and female.' And he said, 'This explains why a man leaves his father and mother and is joined to his wife, and the two are united into one. Since they are no longer two but one, let no one split apart what God has joined together.'
(Matthew 19:3-6)

God's plan for your marriage is that it will last forever and that it will be the most fulfilling human relationship in your life. Given what we are faced with today, you may be asking, "Is it even possible for my marriage to last forever, much less be the most fulfilling relationship in my life?" It is possible. Your marriage can survive – even thrive – but it takes some work. You can't coast through your marriage and expect it to remain strong. You have to open your eyes to the things you can do to keep your relationship moving along the right track.

When I stood before my family, friends and God at my wedding, I made some very strong, specific commitments to my wife. But like most grooms, I really didn't have any idea what I was getting into. I had no clue what it actually took, besides love, to make a marriage work. I didn't have the tools I needed to survive…and neither did you on your wedding day. Thankfully, in navigating my own marriage and in working with hundreds of couples to strengthen theirs, I have been able to identify

God's plan for your marriage is that it will last forever and that it will be the most fulfilling human relationship in your life.

five tools (and their unique respective purposes) that we all need to put in our toolbox to ensure that our marriages are still healthy and happy on our golden anniversary.

THE MARRIAGE SURVIVAL KIT

Tool #1
Alarm Clock – Schedule Time for One Another

Modern Americans work an average of 11 hours more per week than Americans did 20 years ago. We are an achievement-crazed culture. On top of work, we have countless other commitments. Suffice it to say, we don't have a lot of free time to play with. So, especially when you have children, carving out time that's dedicated to your spouse can be tough – but making the effort is well worth it. The number one gift you can give your spouse is quality time.

If you've ever gardened, you may know that a rose bush can survive for a long time on just a little bit of water. But to make a rose bush grow – to cause it to blossom into what God created it to be – you have to give it quite a lot of water. Lack of water won't kill the bush; it will just keep it from flourishing. The same is true of time in your marriage. You may be able to get by without spending quality time with your spouse for years, but you will not have a flourishing relationship.

The first and best way to make quality time with your spouse a priority is to put it on your calendar just as you would anything else that is important to you. Start by scheduling a weekly date night so that you and your spouse can get some quality "couple" time in. Hire a babysitter and go out to dinner, or send the kids to a neighbor and cook dinner together. Take the time to reconnect. For my wife and me, every Thursday night is date night. We may both be barreling busily in different directions Monday through Wednesday, but we know that on Thursday night we've set time aside just for each other. I highly recommend making date night a regular part of your schedule.

Secondly, consider scheduling intimacy with your spouse. Yes, I mean schedule sex. You may push back a little on this idea, but stay with me. In our day, we have this idea that sex with our partner is supposed to "just happen;" that we are to be romantically swept into it, candles, rose petals and all. But in reality, things don't usually work out that way. Life gets busy. We are tired. The kids have a lot of homework. Your spouse gets called in to work. And all of a sudden another day, week or month is gone and the two of you haven't shared any intimacy.

A widely-read article on a popular website recently dove into the idea of scheduling sex.[3] The article says that scheduling sex is important for many reasons. First of all, it eliminates the "ask/beg." No explanation needed. Secondly, instead of feeling unromantic, scheduling sex can feel just the opposite. Planning for it increases desire. You know that it's going to happen, so you think about it. The anticipation builds. And you don't have to go through the whole "is it going to happen/is it not going to happen" dance. One note of caution the article gives is to make sure you put scheduled sex on your calendar in code. That will help you avoid some potentially embarrassing situations!

Planning also helps you give this intimate time with your spouse the attention it deserves. When we let sex fall into the crevices of life, it doesn't get our highest focus. We may be run down or distracted. We may have forgotten to shave. When you plan in advance, you can be ready to give the best of yourself to your mate. So, while scheduling sex may sound rigid at first, it has a lot of benefits. When you use this technique well, it just makes things in the bedroom better. Neglecting this important part of your marriage, on the other hand, can lead to a multitude of problems. (For more tips and teaching on strengthening your marriage, check out www.BeUnshakable.com.)

Tool #2
Rose-Colored Glasses – See the Best in One Another

You've probably heard how important it is to accept your spouse "warts and all." That may sound like silly advice, but it is actually quite biblical. You are called to love your spouse, despite his or her imperfections. In a letter to believers in Ephesus, Paul wrote:

> *Always be humble and gentle. Be patient with each other, making allowance for each other's faults because of your love.* (Ephesians 4:2)

Paul's words are pertinent to every relationship we have in life. To foster the most successful marriage possible, though, we need to take it a step beyond simply overlooking each other's faults. In marriage, there are three levels of love:

Love Level One: I *want to change my spouse. I want to eradicate their faults.* This is immature love.

Love Level Two: I *will look past my spouse's faults. I will love them despite the fact that they're not perfect.* This is good, as noted, but it's not the highest level of love.

Love Level Three: I *will always try to see my spouse in the best possible light. I will look for the positive and not the negative.* This is an expression of the highest level of love in marriage.

I recently heard about a study that backs up the fact that Love Level Three leads to better marriages. Researchers studied the marriages of couples that rated themselves as happy after many years together. They found that the most successful and happiest marriages are those in which each spouse has a higher opinion of their mate than the mate has of themselves. In short, they concluded that the most important quality in a successful marriage is the ability of each spouse to focus on the good in the other.

Oscar Wilde once said, "Marriage is the triumph of imagination over intelligence." Maybe he was getting at this principle. Seeing the good in our mate comes naturally when we are in the throws of infatuation and early love. But as marriage breeds familiarity between us, keeping that same perspective is largely a choice. Every human being is a combination of positive and negative attributes. When it comes to our spouse, we get to choose which attributes to focus on. Here's a little tip: The attributes you focus on are generally the ones that will rise to the top.

When my wife and I were on our honeymoon – the day after we were married, actually – we got into a little fender bender. I thought it was the other driver's fault; he thought it was mine. When the police officer arrived, he saw things my way, which made the other guy furious. In his anger, this guy turned to my wife and said, "You just married this man, right?" She said, "Yes." Then he pointed at me and said, "How does it feel to have just married a liar?" At that, my wife jumped up, put her finger in the guy's face and said, "My husband is not a liar! He's the most honest person I have ever met and you better not say that again!" She was on fire. The police officer actually had to ask me to "take my wife back to the car and leave."

My wife was wearing rose-colored glasses that day. I'm not the most honest person in the world, but knowing she saw me that way made me want to be more honest. As Goethe once taught, "The way you see people is the way you treat them, and the way you treat them is what they become." Husbands, you can actually shape your spouse's behavior in a positive way by looking for the best in her and treating her accordingly. Find the beauty in your spouse even when she doesn't see it in herself. And wives, vice versa.

The Song of Songs is the Bible's most romantic book. In essence, it is a love letter between two young lovers. The letter recounts the lovers' views of one another in this way:

> **Young Man:** *Like a lily among thistles is my darling among young women.*

> **Young Woman:** *Like the finest apple tree in the orchard is my lover among other young men.* (Song of Songs 2:2-3)

Choose to see your spouse as head and shoulders above everyone else.

Tool # 3
White Flag – Surrender the Fight to be Right

Do not panic if you and your spouse fight. No marriage can exist in perpetual harmony. There will be misunderstandings and conflict. That's OK. In fact, when two people agree on everything, one of them isn't necessary. As Alan Patrick Herbert said, "The conception of two people living together for 25 years without having a cross word suggests a lack of spirit only to be admired in sheep." Since arguments are inevitable, the key is to learn when it's OK to argue and when it's not.

My wife and I tend to argue over the smallest things. Can you relate? The majority of our fights aren't over big decisions or future hopes and dreams, but over mundane nothingness. Over the years I've learned that when it comes to arguing over the small things, you have a choice: You can choose to be right or you can choose to be happy. Notice what 2 Timothy 2:14 and 2:23 say about petty arguments:

> *Remind everyone about these things, and command them in God's presence to stop fighting over words. Such arguments are useless, and they can ruin those who hear them. ... Again I say, don't get involved in foolish, ignorant arguments that only start fights.*

I don't know about you, but I need to write those verses down and keep them where I can see them every day.

Humility is the underlying issue when it comes to surrendering your right to be right. When you are humble, you don't have to be right all the time. You don't have to win every battle. You are able to admit when you are wrong. When you feel your temper rising over a little thing, just pause and ask yourself if that thing is worth a fight; if it's worth ruining your day. If it's not, then be humble enough to be the one to bow out of the scuffle. Surrender your right to prove that you are right. Being able to do that actually makes you the winner.

In 1 Corinthians 13:4-7, the greatest chapter on love in the Bible, Paul writes:

> *Love is patient and kind. Love is not jealous or boastful or proud or rude. It does not demand its own way. It is not irritable, and it keeps no record of being wronged. It does not rejoice about injustice but rejoices whenever the*

truth wins out. Love never gives up, never loses faith, is always hopeful, and endures through every circumstance.

Those are wise words for us to live by in our love relationships. If we can learn to give away love that is patient and kind, not jealous or proud or boastful or rude or irritable; if we can love in a way that causes us to never keep records of wrongs (that's a big one, isn't it?); if we can learn to walk in love that never loses faith and is always hopeful; if we can learn to live a love that endures through every circumstance, then we will have cultivated a love that will allow our marriages to thrive fabulously.

Tool #4
Bottle of Repellant – Shut the Door on Temptation

Like pesky ants or cockroaches, temptation comes at us from every corner. It is always lurking in the shadows, just waiting for the right time to make itself known. Our culture is filled with temptations – eat this, buy that, look at her, sleep with him. In the war against your marriage, you need to learn to take this most vital step on a daily basis: Shut the door on sexual temptation. Repel it before it has the chance to infest your relationship.

The enemy would love nothing more than to destroy the union you entered into before God. So he is constantly sending temptation your way. Any of us can be tempted; none of us is immune. When I first got married, I thought that was the end of temptation. After all, I had found the woman I wanted to spend the rest of my life with. I loved her more than words and she was so beautiful – but I quickly learned that temptation doesn't leave you alone just because you put a wedding band on your finger. Sometimes, as is Satan's plan, taking a step of commitment makes temptation even worse. Since we are all tempted, and that's not likely to change on this earth, we have to learn how to handle temptation.

The Bible tells us that sin crouches at the door of every marriage; it is hanging out in the shadows ready and willing to take you down at any moment. If you think you are immune to temptation, take a look at Paul's words in 1 Corinthians 10:12-13:

> *If you think you are standing strong, be careful not to fall.*
> *The temptations in your life are no different from what*
> *others experience...*

No one stands at the altar and plans to have an affair or to become addicted to Internet pornography, yet these things happen every day. Why? Because people don't plan not to. They play with fire and end up getting burned. They make a series of small decisions that ultimately lead to a catastrophe. They tiptoe too close to the edge of morality and then, with the slightest push, they fall off of the cliff. Get the picture?

So, what's the answer? How do you shut the door on sexual temptation and protect your marriage? Look what Paul writes in 1 Corinthians 6:18:

> *Run from sexual sin! No other sin so clearly affects the*
> *body as this one does. For sexual immorality is a sin*
> *against your own body.*

Run! Run away! When you see sexual temptation in the distance, run! It's no coincidence that this is one of the few times a biblical writer uses an exclamation point. Do whatever you have to do to get away from temptation.

There's nothing more important than your marriage and your family. So, if there's someone at work who is causing you to fall into temptation, run. If someone in your neighborhood is tempting you, run. If someone at your gym piques your interest in a sexual way, find a new gym. Do not play with sexual temptation. You have a responsibility to do everything in your power to protect your marriage and your spouse at all costs. Guarding your life against sexual temptation will go a long way toward ensuring that you don't end up as another infidelity statistic.

I know that some of you may be thinking, "Oh, but you don't know me. That will never happen to me." It can happen to you as easily as it can happen to anyone else. Let me repeat the verse from 1 Corinthians 10:12, this time from The Message translation of the scripture: "Don't be so naive and self-confident. You're not exempt. You could fall flat on your face as easily as anyone else...." The more confident you are that it won't happen to you, the harder Satan will work to make you fall. Don't let it happen. At the first sign of temptation, run!

> *Infidelity doesn't just happen. Sexual addictions don't just happen. You have a choice every day to live in a way that protects your marriage.*

Practically speaking, this means that you don't talk to a person of the opposite sex about your problems or your personal life. It means you don't take a second look when you pass an attractive person on the street. It means you block sexual-oriented sites on your computer, if you need to, or get an accountability partner to help you stay away from them. You've got to draw a hard line in the sand and say, "I am choosing to build a wall of protection around myself and my spouse. I am repelling sexual temptation. I am closing the door on potential dangers to my marriage." So many people who fall to sexual temptation default to the excuses, "I didn't mean to" or "I didn't have a choice."

Infidelity doesn't just happen. Sexual addictions don't just happen. You have a choice every day to live in a way that protects your marriage. Run!

But what happens if you've already faced infidelity in your marriage? What if you are dealing with your spouse's or your own failings right now? Deciding how to handle the aftermath if one of you does fall to sexual temptation is also an important discussion. In the Bible, Jesus says that infidelity is grounds for divorce, but he never says that you *should* divorce because of infidelity. As hurtful as this situation can be, you don't have to give up on your marriage.

Recent studies show that two thirds of married couples who decided to stay together and try to make it through infidelity were happy after five years.[4] Why should you try to stay together at all costs? Because your marriage is sacred to God. He wants to protect your marriage, and a mistake on your part doesn't change that. He doesn't throw his hands up and say, "Well, that one's over!" No, he still sees your marriage as holy, and he wants to heal it.

If the offending spouse is willing to ask for forgiveness, change his or her ways and recommit to the relationship, you have to ask yourself if you can, with God's strength, accept that. If the answer is yes, do the hard work of putting things back together. But even more importantly, shut the door on temptation on the front end and spare yourself and your spouse the harm and pain that infidelity causes.

Tool #5
Compass and Map – Set the Spiritual Direction for Your Marriage

When you get married, both you and your spouse choose to serve something – you make something the master of your relationship. Perhaps you each continue to serve yourselves and see marriage as an arrangement where your spouse's job is to make you happy. Maybe you and your spouse have decided to serve money, your careers or your family. Whatever it is, you are serving something. If you want to have a marriage that goes beyond just surviving to having one that thrives, you and your spouse must choose to serve God. Setting the spiritual direction of your marriage toward God is one of the most important marital decisions you can make.

What does serving God together look like? At its base level, you each have to decide individually to make God and his son, Jesus, your foundation. Then, as a couple, you move in his direction together by:

- *Praying Together.* Praying together is truly one of the secrets to a strong marriage. There's an old cliché that says, "Couples who pray together stay together!" As cheesy as it may sound, it became a cliché because statistics prove it to be overwhelmingly true. You don't have to pray long, drawn-out prayers where you say all the names of God in Hebrew. Just say a simple prayer in the morning or before you go to bed at night. Reach over and grab your spouse's hand and ask God to bless your marriage. Have you ever asked him to do that?

- *Reading the Bible Together.* It's important that you read the Bible on your own, but it's also important to incorporate it into the fabric of your marriage. When you need wisdom on a difficult situation – whether it's dealing with money wisely, handling a tough relationship or coping with an illness – go to the Bible together and search out the answer. Doing devotional studies together (or at least at the same time) is also great. You'll be able to talk with each other about what you are learning. (Go to www.BeUnshakable.com for some Bible study suggestions.)

- **Going to Church Together.** Make it a priority to be in church together on a regular basis. You'll learn more about faith and about Scripture, plus you'll have the chance to worship with other like-minded people.

- **Being in a Small Group Together.** One of the best ways you can make a commitment to pointing your marriage in the right direction is by being around other couples who are doing the same. Find a biblically grounded Small Group of couples through your local church and take the sometimes-scary step of joining. You will make new friends, learn about God and strengthen you marriage all at the same time.

Take a look at this triangle:

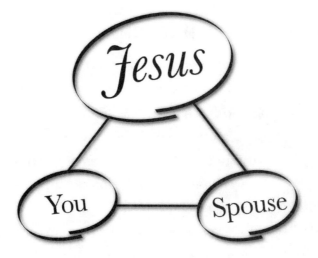

The key to having a strong marriage is to recognize that you and your spouse are not the only ones involved – Jesus is part of your marriage, too. He has sanctified marriage as holy. Think of your marriage in terms of the triangle above. The closer you and your spouse move toward Jesus individually, the closer you move toward each other. The further away you slide from him, the further you slide from each other.

How does this work? Well, the more you become like Jesus, the more you're going to treat your spouse the way Jesus wants you to treat her. The more deeply you fall in love with Jesus and receive love from him, the more love you'll have to give to your spouse. If both of you are becoming more like Christ, your marriage is going to get stronger. You will become closer to God and to your spouse.

Note one more thing about the geometry of the triangle – if one of you is moving toward God while the other is moving away, you will be as far apart from one another as you can get. Set your spiritual direction toward the peak of the triangle and then move that way, both individually and as a couple.

HARD TIMES WILL HAPPEN

From triangles back to rose bushes…marriages are actually a lot like the roses I mentioned earlier. They are beautiful gifts from God, but they come with a few thorns, as all human relationships do. Every married couple could find a reason to call the whole thing off. Even marriages that are a week old can find grounds for a divorce. The key is to continue to find grounds for staying together. Don't be surprised or give up when hard times come, because they will come.

Don't be surprised or give up when hard times come, because they will come.

More marriages would survive if the partners realized that the best times often come after the worst times. Struggles make us stronger, individually and as a unit. So, decide now that you aren't going to let tough times make you want to jump overboard. No matter how things might feel in the midst of the storm, God wants to bless your marriage – and God's blessing comes to those who persevere.

Marriage gives you the opportunity to grow into the person God wants you to be, in partnership with the person you love. When you apply God's plan to your marriage, you will find that marriage is a joy, full of hope and bright futures. But you have to make the choice to love. That's right, love is a choice. Just as God chose to love us, we can choose daily to love our spouse in the same way. When we do, our marriages will be better than we could have ever imagined.

CHAPTER 5

CAREER

Facing Career Challenges With Faith

Everything comes to him who hustles while he waits.
—Thomas Edison

Work willingly at whatever you do, as though
you were working for the Lord rather than for people.
—Colossians 3:23

When you were 8 years old and adults asked you what you wanted to be when you grew up, what did you say? How closely does that answer match your current work situation? Most of us don't end up becoming what we dreamed of as children. Instead, we get carried along the stream of a "wise" or "stable" career track, in search of advancement and security, until we wash up on a shore we never saw coming. We often end up frustrated, burnt out and dissatisfied. Sometimes career problems come because we are focusing our energy on the wrong priorities, and sometimes they creep up because we are tied to a career that doesn't really suit who we are. Either way, these professional storms are difficult to weather.

If you feel like you are being tossed around and beaten up by career challenges, you need to step back and evaluate what's going on from two perspectives:

1) Analyze the true *motives* behind the work you do. In other words, what definition of success drives your actions in the workplace?

2) Examine your personal *makeup* in relation to your career or job situation. How are you uniquely wired and how does that mesh with the career path you are on?

MOTIVES: HOW DO YOU DEFINE SUCCESS?

Your definition of success will not only determine your overall career path but also your daily performance on the job. If you define success by position, you will do all you can to advance through the ranks of your company. If you define success by income, you may do whatever it takes – ethically or otherwise – to increase your bottom line. If you define success by power, you may manipulate the people and situations around you in an attempt to gain control. If you define success by fame, you'll devise all sorts of plans to get your name spoken around America's dinner tables.

Since your definition of success drives your career – and you probably spend anywhere from 40 to 110 hours every week working

– then it is safe to say that your definition of success will influence your entire life. That makes for a pretty important definition. So, consider the question: How do you define success for yourself? Perhaps more importantly, how do you know if your definition is right? Is there a definitive measure? What if you continue pursuing your vision of success only to get to the end of your life and realize that you didn't have the definition right – that your pursuit was empty?

As with most philosophical questions, the Bible can give us some guidance on establishing a strong definition of personal success. First of all, it tells us that success is not defined by what we can see – that is, by the external things of society. Strangely, most of us default to thinking that it is. Jesus warns us:

> *Beware! Guard against every kind of greed. Life is not measured by how much you own.* (Luke 12:15)

Clear enough! What we own is not a measuring stick for the success of our lives. And even though most of us would agree to that truth, we still live like our possessions are the barometer. We think that if we have more than everyone else – if we have the best, the newest, the most expensive toy/car/clothes/fill in the blank – then we are successful. We win. But Jesus says that's not how life is measured.

In 2 Corinthians 3:5, Paul gives us another hint for our working definition of success:

> *It is not that we think we are qualified to do anything on our own. Our qualification comes from God.*

An alternate translation of Paul's words replaces "qualification" with "power and success." He is saying that success as defined by most human standards is a skewed goal. Success isn't about what we can get for ourselves, in our own power. Rather, real success comes from God. Success isn't about external things; it's about an internal attitude.

Success will look slightly different for each and every one of us. But even though your individual definition of success may be different than my definition, God gives us principles that work together to inhabit all true success. By asking these three questions, you can get to the heart of your best path to success:

1. Are you serving others?

Ralph Waldo Emerson once wrote, "It is one of the most beautiful compensations of life, that no man can sincerely try to help another without helping himself." Emerson understood that helping others is good for your soul. What he may not have realized is that the level to which you are willing to serve other people will determine the level of your ultimate success.

"Servant" is the word most associated with success in the Bible. Today, however, the word "servant" sounds radical to us. We don't live in a culture that focuses on selfless service – and service is by definition selfless. Instead, most of us are taught to grab all we can in this "dog eat dog" world. Whether we admit it or not, we usually think in terms of, "What's in it for me?" The servant, on the other hand, asks of those around him, "What would you like? What can I do to help you out?" He puts other people and their needs before himself and his own.

Jesus' disciples were as concerned with success as we are. They were known to talk frequently among themselves about which one of them was the greatest. They competed with each other for recognition and accolades. They each wanted to be the guy to sit at Jesus' right hand in the Kingdom of Heaven. Jesus had to constantly remind them that power is not about position or popularity, but about service. In Matthew 23:11-12, he says it this way:

> *The greatest among you must be a servant. But those who exalt themselves will be humbled, and those who humble themselves will be exalted.*

In our quest for success, we have to cultivate the ability to humble ourselves and serve others. Success is not measured by salary, but by service. If you want to be great, serve as many people as possible. (For ideas on how you can proactively serve others, visit www.BeUnshakable.com.)

2. Are you growing others?

Are you known as the type of person who builds other people up or tears them down? Do you respect other people enough to want them to reach their potential? Do people feel encouraged after they have spent time with you? Your answer to these questions will let you know how well you are growing others. You and I have a basic responsibility to help the people around us become better human beings. As Goethe said, "If you treat an individual as he is, he will stay as he is; but if you treat him as if he were what he ought to be and could be, he will become what he ought to be and could be." There is power in your perspective of and interaction with the people around you.

"Try not to become a person of success, but rather try to become a person of value."
- Albert Einstein

The best way to grow others is to take Jesus' most important command to heart and then live it out in your day-to-day dealings with people. When Jesus was asked to pinpoint the greatest commandment of all, this is what he said:

> *You must love the Lord your God with all your heart, all your soul, and all your mind. This is the first and greatest commandment. A second is equally important: Love your neighbor as yourself.* (Matthew 22:37-39)

If you make the choice to intentionally love God and love people, you will grow the people who cross your path. Your example of service and encouragement will impact them, even if you don't always see the result right away.

Interestingly enough, when you help others grow, God uses the experience to grow you. This is what Jesus was talking about when he said:

> *Give, and you will receive. Your gift will return to you in full – pressed down, shaken together to make room for more, running over, and poured into your lap. The amount you give will determine the amount you get back.*
> (Luke 6:38)

Take an interest in helping people become better, show them love when they may not deserve it, invest in their future, share what you know about faith and support them in their spiritual journey. As you do those things for others, God will grow you in return. The more you give, the more you will grow. Since spiritual growth and true success go hand in hand, this is a success principle worth practicing. As Albert Einstein, a Christian himself, once said, "Try not to become a person of success, but rather try to become a person of value."

3. Are you expanding God's plan?

Success comes when you are more interested in doing God's will and accomplishing his work than in doing things your own way. That is, when God's plan for your life and for your circle of influence takes the number one slot on your priority list. You may be wondering what God's plan is and how you can make it your top priority. Well, just refer back to questions one and two. God's plan is for you to serve others and help them grow closer to him. If that is your number one agenda, then you will be firmly rooted in true success.

Here's a challenge: Tomorrow morning, write the words "God's will" at the top of your to-do list. If you schedule your day in a Blackberry or iPhone, insert "God's will" at the top of your calendar. Let the call to expand God's plan resonate with you as you go about your daily business. It will change the way you interact with those around you, and ultimately put your pursuit of success on a better trajectory.

Thomas Wolfe once wrote, "You have reached the pinnacle of success as soon as you become uninterested in money, compliments or publicity." The best-selling author John Maxwell added, "True success is obeying God." When you obey God by making his plan your motivation and then act on that plan by consciously serving others and helping them grow spiritually, he will make you successful in everything you do. If your definition of success is rooted in this truth, you will never have to worry about coming up empty at the end of your career.

MAKEUP: WHAT KIND OF WORK ARE YOU WIRED FOR?

Once you have analyzed your motives in the workplace and derived the true definition of success, spend some time evaluating your makeup as it relates to your current work situation. In other words, consider how God wired you and how that affects your career.

Gone are the days when people used to work in one profession or for one company for their entire career. In our culture, we are constantly reinventing ourselves. We put a lot of time and effort into deciding "what we want to be," both initially and later on, as our career goals and overall desires evolve. By pulling back the curtain and discovering how God actually wired you, you'll be able to choose your career more effectively, thereby avoiding some intense storms.

God says that if you need wisdom all you have to do is ask:

> *If you need wisdom, ask our generous God, and he will give it to you. He will not rebuke you for asking.*
> (James 1:5)

God is eager to give you his wisdom. Keeping that in mind, ask yourself (and God) these four questions:

1. What does God want?

Hopefully you have matured enough to realize that life is not about you. God's purposes extend far beyond your personal concerns. It makes sense, then, that you would ask, "What does God want for my life?" After all, he is the one who created you. He is the one who chose the parents you were born to, the country you were born in and the opportunities you had access to. He controlled all of these factors because he has a specific plan for your life. So ask him what it is, and then listen for his answer.

Jim Collins, author of the New York Times Bestseller *Good to Great*, begins his insightful business book with this sentence: "Good is the enemy of great." You may be able to do lots of good things with your life, but if you are operating outside of God's will, you won't find your "greatest" life. Good will keep you from great. God wants you to have the best life possible, in him. The plans that he has in store for you are great! Don't trade them for a "good" life apart from him. In light of history, your life is like a vapor. The way to make your years on this earth the absolute best and most meaningful they can be is to align yourself with God's will for your life. (For additional teaching on God's will, check out www. BeUnshakable.com.)

2. What are you good at?

God has given you natural talents and abilities. Examine your life and ask yourself what you are good at. What do other people tell you you're good at? What are your strongest skills? Do others agree? Don't deceive yourself and imagine that you are better at something than you actually are, but take a close, objective look at what kind of talents, skills and abilities surface in your life on a regular basis. How could those things translate into a career?

I grew up with a guy named John. He was a great golfer. He was wired for it. He played all through junior high and high school and then went to college on a golf scholarship. After college, he went on to have some success as an amateur golfer. But John soon realized that he couldn't make a living out of the game he loved.

So here's what he did: John examined the skill set that he used on the golf course – the analytical way of thinking, the ability to predict outcomes and so on – and came to the conclusion that many of those skills would translate well into the business world. So he decided to get a degree in corporate finance. Now he uses the skills that he has been naturally blessed with to run a very successful business.

God wired you to do something really well. What is that something? He created you with a purpose in mind. Try to find the point where your passion and your profession can cross paths. If you find that sweet spot, you will be in a career you love for the rest of your life. Think about what you enjoy and what you are good at, and then analyze those things in light of your current work situation. Are you living out the right fit or do you need to make a change? Don't waste time doing something that God didn't prepare, or wire, you for. As Jesus said:

> For we are God's masterpiece. He has created us anew in
> Christ Jesus, so we can do the good things he planned for
> us long ago. (Ephesians 2:10)

3. What is right in front of you?

Too many people ignore the opportunities right in front of them because they are looking for opportunity to come wearing a different guise. They are waiting for their ship to come in, so they miss the limousine that pulls up beside them, so to speak. You have to be faithful and diligent to do what is in front of you right now. God may ultimately have a different plan in mind for your life, but he has put you where you are today for a reason. He will place stepping stones in your path to get you where you are supposed to go, but only as you do what needs to be done in the present. The things in front of you today may be there specifically to shape you into the person you need to be to fulfill his plan for your life down the road. In Ecclesiastes, God says:

Whatever your hand finds to do, do it with all your might. (Ecclesiastes 9:10, NASB)

Paul echoes the sentiment in his letter to the Colossian church. He writes:

The greatest leaders in every area of the business world are the greatest servers.

Work willingly at whatever you do, as though you were working for the Lord rather than for people. (Colossians 3:23)

Work as if you were working directly for God, rather than for profit, applause or popularity. As you do, he will guide your steps. If you are faithful in the small things, you'll be given more.

4. What is your life's service?

As we established above, success and significance are found through serving other people. In thinking about how you are wired, understand that the ultimate gauge for your life isn't the salary you pull down, but how many people you serve and how well. When you view your life and your purpose through the lens of service, things begin to fall into the proper perspective.

Building your life on the solid foundation of God means that your life's work doesn't need to be about accomplishing goals and increasing profits, but about honoring

God's plan. Now don't get me wrong – you can still accomplish your professional goals and create lots of profit, but those things are not the driving factor of your life when you see things through God's eyes. Instead, what looks like ultimate success to the world will come to you as a byproduct of your service to others. The greatest leaders in every area of the business world are the greatest servers.

Think back to Jesus' commandment: Love God and love people (Matthew 22:37-39). That's exactly what Jesus wired you to do. When you begin to examine your strengths, talents and the work that is in front of you in light of loving God and loving people, you will be on your unique path to true success. (For more detailed teaching on succeeding in the workplace, visit www.BeUnshakable. com.)

CHAPTER 6

DOUBT

Facing Doubt With Faith

The only limit to our realization of tomorrow
will be our doubts of today.
—Franklin D. Roosevelt

Anything is possible if a person believes.
—Jesus

I have a good friend and colleague who had the unique experience of playing football at the college level. As we all know, sports are often analogous to life. In describing coming to terms with doubts, my friend likes to tell this story:

"It was early September 1995 and tiny Furman University (2,500 students) sent its football team, of which I was a member, to Atlanta to play the mighty Georgia Tech Yellow Jackets. This was the opening game for Georgia Tech – a Top 25 team. It was going to be broadcast live up and down the east coast on ABC Sports. Perhaps needless to say, we were predicted to lose. Actually, more than lose, we were supposed to get crushed...

"But our coach told us that we had to have faith that we could win the game. In fact, he told us we could have no doubts. He said that if we had doubts, we definitely wouldn't win. So our team mantra for the match up became, 'No doubt!'

"When we took the field that September afternoon in front of 70,000 people, plus the thousands watching on television, we had no doubt that we could beat Georgia Tech. And when we saw Georgia Tech run onto the field – when we saw how big they were – we still had no doubt. When we kicked off to start the game and they fumbled the return and we recovered, we definitely had no doubt. Then, when we drove down and kicked a field goal and went ahead 3 to nothing, we had no doubt whatsoever.

"Even when they drove down the field and scored on the next kick off, we still had no doubt. Then they got the ball back and drove down again to make the score 14 to 3. At that point, a little doubt started to creep in. Then they drove again and went ahead 21 to 3. The doubt was starting to mount. After they scored their eighth consecutive touchdown to go ahead 56 to 3, and it was still the third quarter, doubt doesn't even begin to describe what we were feeling.

"You know, faith comes easily when our lives are going well. But when challenges start to show up, they often bring doubts with them. When we are down 56 to 3 in life, doubt often starts undermining our faith. It can really shake us to our core. That's why it is so important to learn to stand strong against the doubts that come into our lives..."

What kind of doubts do you struggle with? Do you have doubts that are keeping you from taking steps in your career? Do you have doubts about relationships that cause you to put walls up around yourself? Do you have doubts about God that keep you from being able to trust him? Doubts are powerful. If we let them, they will rob us of living our best life. But completely avoiding them isn't an option. They invade our consciousness uninvited. So, what can we do to keep doubts from taking control of our emotions and our actions? We have to learn to face doubts fully grounded on a solid foundation of faith.

A COMMON CONUNDRUM

Everyone struggles with doubt. Even the wisest spiritual teachers have wrestled with their own doubts about the nature of God and their place in the world. Such doubts are simply part of our human condition. The imperfect world we live in is a doubt breeding ground – especially when it comes to faith in God.

Take a look at the following passage from the New Testament, but first allow me to set the scene... Jesus has just been on a mountaintop with his three closest disciples, Peter, James and John. They have had a tremendous spiritual experience (read about it in Mark 9:2-13), but as soon as they come down off of the mountain, back into the valley of real life, they find a mess:

When they returned to the other disciples, they saw a large crowd surrounding them, and some teachers of religious law were arguing with them. When the crowd saw Jesus, they were overwhelmed with awe, and they ran to greet him.

'What is all this arguing about?' Jesus asked.

One of the men in the crowd spoke up and said, 'Teacher, I brought my son so you could heal him. He is possessed by an evil spirit that won't let him talk. And whenever this spirit seizes him, it throws him violently to the ground. Then he foams at the mouth and grinds his teeth and becomes rigid. So I asked your disciples to cast out the evil spirit, but they couldn't do it.'

Jesus said to them, 'You faithless people! How long must I be with you? How long must I put up with you? Bring the boy to me.'

So they brought the boy. But when the evil spirit saw Jesus, it threw the child into a violent convulsion, and he fell to the ground, writhing and foaming at the mouth.

'How long has this been happening?' Jesus asked the boy's father.

He replied, 'Since he was a little boy. The spirit often throws him into the fire or into water, trying to kill him. Have mercy on us and help us, if you can.'

'What do you mean, If I can?' Jesus asked. 'Anything is possible if a person believes.'

The father instantly cried out, 'I do believe, but help me overcome my unbelief!'

When Jesus saw that the crowd of onlookers was growing, he rebuked the evil spirit. 'Listen, you spirit that makes this boy unable to hear and speak,' he said. 'I command you to come out of this child and never enter him again!'

Then the spirit screamed and threw the boy into another violent convulsion and left him. The boy appeared to be dead. A murmur ran through the crowd as people said, 'He's dead.' But Jesus took him by the hand and helped him to his feet, and he stood up.

Afterward, when Jesus was alone in the house with his disciples, they asked him, 'Why couldn't we cast out that evil spirit?'

Jesus replied, 'This kind can be cast out only by prayer.'

(Mark 9:14-29)

Let's break this passage down: A concerned father brings his son to the disciples for healing, but the disciples can't do it. Their inability to cast the spirit out of the boy starts a commotion. The religious leaders begin calling the disciples fakes. Doubt starts to enter into the picture – especially for the desperate father. When Jesus steps onto the scene, the father, with his last shred of hope begs, "Heal him, if you can."

That's when Jesus turns the situation on its head and teaches everyone in the vicinity an incredible lesson about doubt. He says, "What do you mean, 'If I can'? Anything is possible if a person believes'" (Mark 9:23). Essentially, Jesus is telling the boy's father, "This has nothing to do with me; I can do anything. This has to do with your faith and with the doubt you are dealing with." To which the father candidly replies, "I do believe, but help me overcome my unbelief!" (Mark 9:24). That simple prayer is one of the most powerful prayers in the Bible. While tinged with doubt, it is also full of faith.

As Jesus goes on to tell the disciples later in the passage, prayer was the key to the boy's healing. The only thing that could overcome the creeping doubt and open the way for Jesus to work was the honest prayer of that father. With this passage in mind, let's take a look at five truths about doubt:

Truth #1
It's easy to have faith on the mountaintop, but it's hard not to doubt in the valley.

When you are on the mountaintop with Jesus – when you are feeling close to him and when things are going well in your life – it's easy to have faith. But when you have to walk back down into the valley of everyday life, doubt will do its best to shadow you.

Truth #2
Doubt is a sign that there is a broken connection with God.

Doubt is a warning sign in your life that something is askew in your relationship with God. Let your doubt point you toward what needs to be fixed.

Truth #3
Doubt limits God's power in my life.

Consider how Jesus turned the situation with the father to make him realize that his own doubt was preventing his son's healing. Jesus reminded the father that "anything is possible if a person believes," (Mark 9:23).

Truth #4
Jesus only requires a small amount of faith.

Jesus knows that our faith is imperfect. He knows that we all struggle with doubts. That's why he only requires a small amount of faith. Jesus goes so far as to say:

> *I tell you the truth, if you had faith even as small as a mustard seed, you could say to this mountain, 'Move from here to there,' and it would move. Nothing would be impossible.* (Matthew 17:20)

The father's imperfect prayer was tinged with doubt, but it also contained a mustard seed of faith; that's all Jesus needed to see.

Truth #5
Prayer is essential to overcoming doubt.

Even though the father's prayer is imperfect, he was at least willing to pray. His prayer connects him with Jesus, and his faith paves the way for his son's healing. In the same way, prayer is essential to our being able to overcome the doubts and obstacles that we face every day.

THE POWER OF PRAYER

Keeping these five truths about doubt in mind, let's take a look at the five most common issues that creep into our lives, drive our own doubts and try to keep us from living a life of faith. You may not have faced all of these situations your life yet, but rest assured, if you live long enough, each one of these "doubt-drivers" will come into your life in some form sooner or later. As we dive in, remember Jesus' words to the disciples in our passage, "This...can be cast out only by prayer" (Mark 9:29).

Doubt-Driver 1
Difficult Circumstances

When difficult circumstances cause doubt, prayer releases God's power into your life.

Difficult circumstances cause people to doubt God. Whether it's an illness, a marriage that's falling apart, the death of a loved one, the loss of a job or whatever difficult situation may arise, too often our first response is to question God. We protest, "God, where are you? How could you allow this to happen to me? Why didn't you stop this?"

Doubt is exactly how the enemy wants you to respond to the difficult circumstances in your life. So when difficulty shows up, Satan's first step is to wedge a dose of doubt between you and God. Then he can use that doubt to continue to push you further and further from God. But God has a different plan. He wants to use the difficult circumstances in your life to draw you closer to him. He wants you to turn to him and rely on his strength.

God wants to use the difficult circumstances in your life to draw you closer to him.

God doesn't cause the difficult circumstances in our lives, but he does allow them. Why? So that you will learn to walk in his power. The pathway to that power is prayer. While difficult circumstances often make us feel powerless, prayer allows us to connect with God and receive his power. That's when his peace and his presence step in and help us deal with the issues we are facing.

Doubt-Driver 2
Intellectual Arguments

When intellectual arguments cause doubt, prayer reminds you of God's presence.

We've all faced friends, family members, professors and colleagues who try to use intellectual arguments to call our faith into question. This is nothing new. Looking back on our story in Mark 9, the religious leaders in the crowd were trying to cause both the father and all of the onlookers to doubt Jesus and his disciples by making arguments against their authenticity. Mark 9:14 says, "Teachers of religious law were arguing with them." As we all know, plenty of people still try to argue the validity of Christianity today. These arguments can plant seeds of doubt in our mind, sometimes even causing us to question our faith.

What these argumentative unbelievers fail to realize is that Christianity is a faith of reason. For Christians, faith and reason don't conflict. Faith and science are not mutually exclusive. Faith, reason and science create a synergistic explanation for the world. For the Christian, science and reason answer the question of how things work, and faith answers the question of why. Faith also openly addresses the issue of where we come from. When you are faced with intellectual arguments that want to shake your faith, remind yourself that Christianity is reasonable. Many of the greatest thinkers in human history were (and are) are followers of Jesus.

Prayer is a critical part of experiencing God's presence and love in our lives. Prayer reminds us of all the times when we have known that God is real and active. It connects us to God's heart and allows us to overcome doubts with faith. No intellectual argument can ever produce doubt that is greater than your own personal experience with God.

Doubt-Driver 3
Imperfect Christians

When imperfect Christians cause doubt, prayer helps you look past them to God's Son.

Many people let their faith get shaken when a Christian friend or acquaintance disappoints them. Again, this is nothing new. Think back to the father in Mark 9. Doubt certainly began to grow in his mind when the disciples weren't able to cast the spirit out of his son. He probably started thinking, "If they can't do it, they must be frauds...which probably means Jesus is a fraud." When those associated with Jesus come up short, our tendency is to doubt Jesus himself.

People who are not standing on a solid foundation will usually jump on any opportunity they see to use other people to cast doubt on Jesus. Why wouldn't they? If those associated with God fall, it makes their disassociation look all the better. There are people who have let the child abuse scandals in the Catholic Church cause them to question faith. Others see an evangelist on TV that they can't relate to and think, "He looks suspicious, so this whole God thing must be suspicious." And, of course, there are many who have been more personally hurt or mistreated by a Christian – or someone who claims to be a Christian – and turn their back on faith as a result.

Have you ever had a problem with your cell phone reception? Of course you have. Did it cause you to throw your phone away and vow never to have anything to do with cell phones again? Of course not. Instead, you acknowledge that the problem is with the receiver or the local reception, not with cell phone technology in general.

Similarly, you can't let an imperfect person, an imperfect pastor or an imperfect church cause you to turn your back on a perfect savior. Christians are human beings, which means that they are imperfect by definition. But Jesus is perfect. So fix your eyes on him instead of on the imperfect Christians around you. Hebrews 12:2 (NASB) tells us that we should be "fixing our eyes on Jesus, the author and perfecter of faith, who for the joy set before Him endured the cross, despising the shame, and has sat down at the right hand of the throne of God."

Prayer is especially important when you are hurt by a Christian or by the church, because when you talk to God you are able to see past earthly imperfections to the perfection of his son. If you put your faith in people, they will eventually let you down – Christian or not. There is no perfect person. There is no perfect organization. Flaws and faults abound. The only person who won't let you down is Jesus Christ himself. Focus on him and what he has done for you; then, your faith won't be shaken by the imperfections around you.

Doubt-Driver 4
Spiritual Dryness

When times of spiritual dryness cause doubt, prayer allows you to hear God's voice.

All believers go through periods of spiritual dryness – those stretches of time when you just don't feel God's presence. You pray, but you don't hear his voice. You feel stranded in a spiritual desert. As one author wrote, "Any relationship involves times of closeness and times of distance. And in a relationship with God, no matter how intimate, the pendulum will swing from one to side to the other."

During these times of spiritual dryness, doubt often begins to creep in. When we aren't hearing from God, sometimes we begin to doubt his love, his plan and even his existence. We feel abandoned. But the truth is that God never abandons us. He has a purpose in the dryness. He wants to draw us closer to himself. He may even be preparing us for something big that he has in store.

When times of dryness come, make sure that you stay connected to God through prayer, even if it is frustrating. That way, you'll be prepared to hear him when he does speak. (For more about staying connected to God through prayer, visit www.BeUnshakable.com.) Though you may feel like God is a long way away, continuing to pray will keep you nourished. Look what King David wrote in Psalm 1:3 about those who are committed to a life of prayer:

> *They are like trees planted along the riverbank, bearing fruit each season. Their leaves never wither, and they prosper in all they do.*

Doubt-Driver 5
Recurring Sins

When recurring sins in your life cause doubt, prayer reveals God's grace.

Have you every felt like you were locked in battle with a recurring sin in your life? You aren't alone. Christians all around you feel the same way. In fact, the Apostle Paul, the greatest Christian missionary to ever live, wrote about this constant struggle with our sin nature:

> *I don't really understand myself, for I want to do what is right, but I don't do it. Instead, I do what I hate. ... Oh, what a miserable person I am! Who will free me from this*

life that is dominated by sin and death? Thank God! The answer is in Jesus Christ our Lord. (Romans 7:15, 24-25)

The more passionately you live for God, the more intense the struggle is going to be. The closer to God you draw, the more the enemy is going to try to throw you off course. But there is good news: As you lean into God through prayer, he will pour his power into your life to help you win the battle. And when sin does get the best of you, as it will from time to time, God will give you grace and forgiveness as soon as you ask him.

These five doubt-drivers will all come into your life at some point. When they sneak in and start trying to tempt you to question your faith, just remember the possessed boy's father from Mark 9 and, as he did, choose to have to have enough faith to ask Jesus for help. Be willing to say, "I do believe, but help me overcome my unbelief." Those words can release God's power in your life. As you learn to move forward through prayer in every doubt-inducing situation, you will be able to stand unshaken in the face of life's storms.

CHAPTER 7

DEATH

Facing the Death of People
We Love With Faith

For death begins with life's first breath,
and life begins at touch of death.
—John Oxenham

O death, where is your victory?
O death, where is your sting?
—Paul

Some of the great comedians of our time have worked to bring a little humor to the difficult subject of death. As George Carlin once put it, "Death is caused by swallowing small amounts of saliva over long periods of time." True enough! Woody Allen famously said, "I'm not afraid to die, I just don't want to be there when it happens." Have you ever felt that way? We all know that death is inevitable; we just don't want to be there when it becomes official. Unfortunately, that's not an option. Throughout this life, we will face death. Loved ones will die. Friends will die. We will die. Death is an inevitable part of life's journey.

Think back to the first time death became a reality for you. Do you remember the moment you realized that death existed in your world? For me, death first made its way into my consciousness when I was 6 years old. One morning, my parents received a phone call that my grandmother had suffered a massive heart attack in her sleep. Even though I was only 6, I knew something was terribly wrong. I watched my upset parents hustle frantically around the house, trying to get ready and get out the door. They dropped me off to spend the day with some relatives, rather than taking me into the situation at my grandmother's house. I didn't even go to the funeral. But I knew that something had changed in my world. Suddenly, death wasn't just for cartoon characters anymore.

As the years went by, I dealt with other losses. I had a cousin who died not long after my grandmother. In high school, a friend of mine committed suicide. More recently, my wife Kelley and I faced a different sort of death. Our pet bulldog – who had been with us for 10 years – died of a brain tumor… Perhaps these experiences bring up memories for you. What type of death have you faced in your life?

The hard truth is that death is extremely difficult, but there's no getting around it. Everything that lives eventually dies. When someone we love dies, we find ourselves in the middle of one of the worst storms life can bring our way. Learning to face death with faith is essential to making it to the other side of the pain. God knows that dealing with death is hard for us, so the Bible offers a lot of guidance.

In 1 Thessalonians 4:13, the Apostle Paul is addressing a group of Christians in Thessalonica who have lost someone close to them. Trying to help them with their grieving, he says:

> *And now, dear brothers and sisters, we want you to know*
> *what will happen to the believers who have died so you*
> *will not grieve like people who have no hope.*

Paul is not supposing that people of faith will not grieve the death of their loved ones – just that we will not grieve like those "who have no hope." Grief and mourning are natural. We mourn the loss of the one who died; we are sad that we have been left behind without them; we are upset over how much we are going to miss them. Paul is not trying to sugarcoat these realities. Rather, he is highlighting the chasm between two different levels of under-standing. That is, for the person whose life is built on a solid foundation of faith, death is tremendously painful but not unbear-able, because we have hope in heaven and assurance that God has a plan; while for the unbeliever, death is accompanied by unbear-able, inordinate sorrow because it really is a final, misunderstood goodbye.

Take a fresh look at Jesus' story about these two types of people. You may remember it from Chapter 1:

> *Anyone who listens to my teaching and follows it is wise,*
> *like a person who builds a house on solid rock. Though*
> *the rain comes in torrents and the floodwaters rise and the*
> *winds beat against that house, it won't collapse because*

*it is built on bedrock. But anyone who hears my teaching
and doesn't obey it is foolish, like a person who builds
a house on sand. When the rains and floods come and
the winds beat against that house, it will collapse with a
mighty crash.* (Matthew 7:24-27)

When your faith is built on the right bedrock, you can face the
worst storms of life – even the death of someone you love – without
being fundamentally shaken. But if you are building on a foundation of sand, you will not be able to stand. When death comes into
your world, you will be like the hopeless mourners Paul refers to
above. Later, in a letter to the Corinthian church, Paul writes:

*For we know that when this earthly tent we live in is taken
down (that is, when we die and leave this earthly body),
we will have a house in heaven, an eternal body made for
us by God himself and not by human hands.*
(2 Corinthians 5:1)

Death is always going to be one of the most painful things you
and I have to face on this earth. But if you anchor your life on faith
in God and let what the Bible teaches about death become part
of your understanding, you will be able to find peace even in the
midst of this most difficult situation. Here are some things you can
do to make sure you are able to face death with unshakable faith:

Turn Immediately to God

In the New Testament, Jesus' disciple James teaches, "Come close
to God, and God will come close to you," (James 4:8). But how is it
possible to "come close to God," especially after someone you love
has just died? Christians throughout the years have struggled with

this question. James is simply telling us that we can draw close to God by admitting our anger and sadness to him, while at the same time acknowledging our need for and dependence on him. When we do that, he will be right there with us.

Charles Spurgeon was the pastor of London's Metropolitan Baptist Tabernacle in the 1800s. During that time, the Tabernacle was the largest church in the world. One fall evening, as Spurgeon was teaching a crowd of about 10,000 people, someone yelled, "fire!" Chaos ensued. In the mad rush to get out of the arena, hundreds of people were injured and seven were killed. Those seven deaths haunted Spurgeon for the rest of his life, as is proven by some of his later writings. For years, he struggled to make sense of what had happened. He didn't know the seven victims personally, but their demise weighed on his soul. Even though he wrestled with God in an attempt to understand, he chose to draw close to him at the same time. In return, God drew close to Spurgeon. Years later, he penned these thoughts about death that have served as an encouragement to people around the globe:

> God is too wise to be mistaken. And God is too good to be unkind. When you can't trace His hand, you can always trust His heart.

If you try to trace the hand of God in the circumstances that lead to the death of a loved one, you will be left distraught and carrying a load that God never intended for you to shoulder. But if you will choose to draw close to him, trusting his heart and acknowledging his goodness, he will draw close to you and become your source of comfort. You will experience God in an entirely new way.

King David faced some big losses in his life. During one particularly difficult season of loss, he wrote some verses you may be familiar with. Many people turn to this passage of Scripture when they are facing the death of someone they love:

> *The Lord is my shepherd, I shall not want. He makes me lie down in green pastures; He leads me beside quiet waters. He restores my soul; He guides me in the paths of righteousness for His name's sake. Even though I walk through the valley of the shadow of death, I fear no evil, for You are with me; Your rod and Your staff, they comfort me. You prepare a table before me in the presence of my enemies; You have anointed my head with oil; My cup overflows. Surely goodness and loving-kindness will follow me all the days of my life, and I will dwell in the house of the Lord forever.* (Psalm 23, NASB)

When you walk through death's shadow, God is walking with you. He's not sitting up in heaven saying, "Oh, I hope they get through this OK." No, he is there every step of the way – to protect you and to give you comfort, assurance and strength. But first you have to draw close to him. Drawing close to God does not mean that the pain will go away immediately, but God will begin to lead you through a process of healing.

Give Yourself Permission to Mourn

Mourning is a natural part of healing. Not only that, it's biblical. There is a time to laugh and a time to cry, a time to dance and a time to grieve. When we lose a loved one, grief and mourning are inevitable, but always in light of the hope of our faith.

Everyone who comes face to face with the death of a loved one will go through similar stages. The author Elisabeth Kubler-Ross most popularly defined these stages in her 1969 book, *On Death and Dying.*[5] Interestingly, the stages of grief as Kubler-Ross describes them closely mirror what the Bible says about how you and I move through the grieving process:

Denial: When someone we love dies, our initial response is to deny it. We don't let ourselves acknowledge the loss. But we can only stay in denial for so long. When the truth finally becomes unavoidable, we move to the next phase.

Anger: Lots of people get angry with God when they lose someone they love. They question why God would let the death happen. While this is understandable given our humanity, let me encourage you to guard against the anger stage. Choose instead to draw close to God. He's the only one who can bring you peace.

Bargaining: In the bargaining stage, we are tempted to exchange our pain for any kind of temporary relief. Too many people turn to substance abuse after a loss. They find some escape as their drug of choice quells the pain – but only momentarily. The problem with this trade off is that the pain always comes back worse than before… which leads to more bargaining, which leads to more pain, which leads to more bargaining. You get the picture.

Depression: Those who are grieving usually feel depression taking its toll anywhere from a few weeks to a couple of months after the death, as they see life around them continuing to go on in the absence of their loved one. This is when the reality of life after loss starts to set in.

Acceptance: Acceptance is the final stage of grieving. Acceptance doesn't mean that you "get over it." You never get over the loss of someone close to you; it just becomes part of the fabric of who you are. Acceptance simply means that you acknowledge that God is in control, and you choose to trust his heart. You allow the death of your loved one to draw you closer to him.

In the acceptance phase, you may even be able to acknowledge that God can use the difficult situation to help others. Jesus once said, "God blesses those who mourn, for they will be comforted" (Matthew 5:4). No one can comfort another person like someone who has been comforted by God. He can take your greatest loss and allow you to be an encouragement to others.

Admit that You Need Support from Others

Don't try to face the days after a friend or family member's death on your own. Grief often makes us feel like closing the door on the rest of the world and looking for respite inside ourselves. Resist the urge. God doesn't intend for us to go through life's difficulties in solitude. We are not wired for it. We need support from others.

You never get over the loss of someone close to you; it just becomes part of the fabric of who you are.

Even Moses, one of the greatest leaders in the Bible, needed support from others to make it through difficult circumstances. In the passage below, Moses is engaged in a battle. God has told him that as long as his arms are raised, his army would have victory, but if his arms were to fall, the army would taste defeat:

While the people of Israel were still at Rephidim, the warriors of Amalek attacked them. Moses commanded Joshua, 'Choose some men to go out and fight the army of Amalek for us. Tomorrow, I will stand at the top of the hill, holding the staff of God in my hand.'

So Joshua did what Moses had commanded and fought the army of Amalek. Meanwhile, Moses, Aaron, and Hur climbed to the top of a nearby hill. As long as Moses held up the staff in his hand, the Israelites had the advantage. But whenever he dropped his hand, the Amalekites gained the advantage. Moses' arms soon became so tired he could no longer hold them up. So Aaron and Hur found a stone for him to sit on. Then they stood on each side of Moses, holding up his hands. So his hands held steady until sunset. (Exodus 17:8-12)

When you are battling through a difficult time in your life, you need people around you who can hold your arms up. In other words, you need people to help you hold on to your hope, hold up your attitude and take hold of your emotions. That's part of the reason God gave us the church. The church is a spiritual family, linked together by a common Father – a family that celebrates with you in good times and helps you get through the difficult times. In Galatians 6:2, Paul tells us how we can encourage one another no matter what we are facing. He writes, "Share each other's burdens, and in this way obey the law of Christ."

Use the Opportunity to Grow and Share Your Faith

When a death occurs, faith inevitably enters the discussion. In my 20 years as a pastor, I have been at the bedside of many dying people. I can tell you, there is a tremendous difference between someone who dies without faith in Jesus Christ and someone who dies with faith. Seeing that divide has motivated me to use the opportunity that death brings with it to talk to people about the reality of eternity. Death gives us a chance to point people toward God and to remind them of the hope that we have in Jesus.

When Paul was facing his own death, he wrote these famous words:

> *For to me, to live is Christ and to die is gain.*
> (Philippians 1:21, NASB)

How could Paul possibly have said that to die would be "gain?" Because when a person who believes in Jesus as their savior passes away, they do gain – they gain heaven, eternity and the presence of Jesus himself. Christianity is not only the best way to live; it's also the best way to die. There really is victory beyond the grave. As 1 Corinthians 15 says:

> *Death is swallowed up in victory. O death, where is your victory? O death, where is your sting?... But thank God! He gives us victory over sin and death through our Lord Jesus Christ.* (1 Corinthians 15:54-55,57)

If we have built our life on a solid foundation of faith, the death of our friends and family members – while not easy, by any means – won't be able to knock us into despair, as it does those with no hope. The storm may rage, but it won't overtake us. Thanks to Jesus, the sting of death has been removed. We can remain unshaken in its presence. (For additional resources on dealing with the death of a loved one, go to www.BeUnshakable.com.)

Conclusion
How to Live With Unshakable Faith

A living faith will last in the midst of the blackest storm.
—Gandhi

Anyone who listens to my teaching and follows it is wise,
like a person who builds a house on solid rock...
But anyone who hears my teaching and doesn't obey
it is foolish, like a person who builds a house on sand.
—Jesus

Not long ago, my wife Kelley, my son Alexander and I were staying in a friend's house. Late one night, after Kelley and Alexander had gone to bed, I decided to make use of my friend's office area to get some work done. As I was settling into the desk chair, I noticed a snake on the ground beside my foot. I froze. Then, doing my best not to disturb it, I slid out of the chair and retreated to the other side of the office. My heart was pounding.

After several deep breaths to clear my head, I slipped out of the room and rummaged around in a few closets until I found a broom. The office had glass doors that opened onto the yard, so my plan was to stun the sucker with the handle of the broom, get those glass doors open and sweep it outside – all without getting bitten. I tiptoed back into the office. Sure enough, the snake was right where I had left him, so I put my plan into action. Stun. Open. Sweep. It worked! Mission accomplished. The bad news was that I was too rattled to get any work done. When I finally calmed down, I headed to bed.

The next morning, I couldn't wait to tell Kelley about how I had saved us all from certain danger. As I poured her a cup of coffee, I said, "You are never going to believe this! There was a snake in the office last night and…"

"Was it a black snake?" she asked.

"Yeah, it was black… I sat down right beside it, but it didn't move. So I eased out of the chair and snuck out of the office and found a broom…"

"Was it about this long?" She held her hands 16 inches or so apart.

"Yes…" I answered, wondering where these questions were coming from. "Anyway, I decided to stun it and then…"

Before I could finish my story, Kelley burst into laughter. I was a little offended.

"Why are you laughing," I asked.

"I bought Alexander that snake at the toy store yesterday!"

I have to admit – I was embarrassed. Here I was thinking of myself as a snake wrangler on par with Indiana Jones, only to find that my nemesis had been a measly piece of plastic and rubber. But the whole scenario got me thinking…

Lots of times, we let things shake us that really don't have to. Situations that seem overwhelming at first are often only child's play. We need to be able to stay calm enough to step back and see things from the right perspective. But, by nature, we default to anxiety even though God tells us not to be anxious about anything:

> *Don't worry about anything; instead, pray about*
> *everything. Tell God what you need, and thank him for*
> *all he has done. Then you will experience God's peace,*
> *which exceeds anything we can understand. His peace*
> *will guard your hearts and minds as you live in Christ*
> *Jesus.* (Philippians 4:6-7)

On the other hand, sometimes situations come into our lives that truly have the potential to shake us to our core. Uncertainty about our future, the death of a loved one, problems with our spouse, an unexpected illness or trouble with our kids are just a few examples of the many things that could throw us off course. As long as we live on this earth, we will have to weather the storms of life. But as we learned in Chapter 1:

> *It is possible to survive the storms of life unscathed if you*
> *have the right foundation.*

No matter what difficult situation you are facing or will face in the future, you can remain unshaken if you have the right foundation of faith. When storms begin to rage in your life, here are a few steps you can take to calm the winds and rain:

Step #1
Make sure you have a strong foundation of faith.

Think back to Jesus' story about the person who builds his life on a solid foundation of faith versus the one who builds on shifting sand. As you'll remember, Jesus says:

> *Anyone who listens to my teaching and follows it is wise,*
> *like a person who builds a house on solid rock. Though*
> *the rain comes in torrents and the floodwaters rise and the*
> *winds beat against that house, it won't collapse because*
> *it is built on bedrock. But anyone who hears my teaching*
> *and doesn't obey it is foolish, like a person who builds*
> *a house on sand. When the rains and floods come and*
> *the winds beat against that house, it will collapse with a*
> *mighty crash.* (Matthew 7:24-27)

The only way to make sure that you are building your life on a solid foundation is to put your faith in Jesus. As he says in the gospels:

> *I am the way, the truth, and the life. No one can come to*
> *the Father except through me.* (John 14:6)

In the same way that Jesus once asked one of his disciples, "Who do you say that I am" (Mark 8:29), he asks you and me the same question. Sooner or later, we all have to make a decision about who we believe he is. Either we accept Jesus as who he says he is, or we reject his teachings and continue to go our own way. Take a look at how C.S. Lewis – a professor at Cambridge University and, at one time, an agnostic – once positioned the options:

I am trying here to prevent anyone saying the really foolish thing that people often say about Him: 'I'm ready to accept Jesus as a great moral teacher, but I don't accept His claim to be God.' That is the one thing we must not say. A man who was merely a man and said the sort of things Jesus said would not be a great moral teacher. He would either be a lunatic – on a level with the man who says he is a poached egg – or else he would be the Devil of Hell. You must make your choice. Either this man was, and is, the Son of God: or else a madman or something worse. You can shut Him up for a fool, you can spit at Him and kill Him as a demon; or you can fall at His feet and call Him Lord and God. But let us not come with any patronizing nonsense about His being a great moral teacher. He has not left that open to us. He did not intend to.[6]

God's desire is that we would see Jesus clearly for who he is and walk the path of true life by accepting him as our savior. In fact, God's plan of salvation is unambiguous and unchanging. Ephesians 1:5 says:

God decided in advance to adopt us into his own family by bringing us to himself through Jesus Christ. This is what he wanted to do, and it gave him great pleasure.

You and I can gain forgiveness for our sins, a relationship with the one who created us, and eternity in heaven, if we accept the salvation that God offers through Jesus.

We have been separated from God because of our sin. (Our sin nature is an ongoing condition we can all admit we wrestle with, if we are honest.) But God sent his son into the world to live a perfect life among us and then to be crucified as a covering for our transgressions. As John 3:16 says:

> *For God loved the world so much that he gave his one and*
> *only Son, so that everyone who believes in him will not*
> *perish but have eternal life.*

Jesus paid the debt for all of our sins when he died on the cross. Three days later, he was resurrected, so that we could receive new life. Now, he calls you and I to accept his free gift of forgiveness and salvation.

MY STORY

I became a follower of Christ a little differently, and a little later, than most people might expect. I asked Jesus to come into my life right around my 18th birthday. Until that point, I had been consumed with some other things. I had started and sold a computer business while I was in high school. When I hit 17, I was working on an engineering degree at North Carolina State University, while traveling and speaking at different conferences for young entrepreneurs.

At one of these conferences, I met a guy who had written a book I wanted to read, so I headed to a local bookstore to pick it up. While I was there, I noticed a book by Billy Graham called *Peace With God.* I bought Dr. Graham's book on a whim, thinking it was a history book about a guy I had heard a little about while growing up in North Carolina.

So, in October of 1989, I was reading through *Peace With God* and got to the page where Billy Graham offered an invitation of salvation to anyone who didn't know Jesus. My heart was convicted. I prayed the prayer that Dr. Graham had written out for me there and then saw a toll-free number that he suggested I call. I went back to my little apartment in Raleigh and called the number. Yep, I'm that guy. The person on the other end of the line suggested I do a few things – read my Bible, pray, get involved in a good church and make my decision public through baptism.

After I gave my life to God, he put me on a new path. I ended up getting my bachelor's degree in religion and psychology at Gardner-Webb University and then a Master of Divinity at Duke University, while pastoring a little church outside of Charlotte, North Carolina. Eventually, I moved to Southern California to work with Rick Warren and the Purpose Driven Community. In 2001, my wife Kelley and I moved to Manhattan to start The Journey Church of the City. Then, in 2010, we moved to Boca Raton, Florida, to start The Journey – Boca.

God is calling you to make the same decision about his son. If you have never asked Jesus to come into your life, let me encourage you to pray the prayer I prayed that fall day in North Carolina:

> *Dear God, I open my heart to you and invite you into my life. I confess that I am a sinner. I ask that you would forgive me of all that I've done wrong. Thank you for sending your son, Jesus, who died for me and who gives me the opportunity to know you. I want to be your follower. Thank you for accepting me. In Jesus' name I pray. Amen*

If you just prayed that prayer from your heart, you are now part of God's family. Congratulations and welcome to the journey! From now on, your life will be built on the solid foundation of faith in Jesus. You can find some materials that will answer your questions and show you what to do next at www.BeUnshakable.com. You've just made the greatest decision of your life!

Step #2
Don't be surprised.

God never said that life on this side of heaven would be easy, even for those who have put their faith in him. We live in a fallen world, full of problems, difficult circumstances and disappointments. In fact, there is a word that describes what it is to face one problem after another: life. As Christians, we need to accept this reality rather than being surprised when difficulties show up. If we can simply acknowledge that pain and trouble are part of life on earth, we won't be so shaken when the storms come.

Thankfully, even when the storms do rage, we know that we have a safe haven to run to. Jesus says:

> *I have told you all this so that you may have peace in me.*
> *Here on earth you will have many trials and sorrows. But*
> *take heart, because I have overcome the world.*
> (John 16:33)

God doesn't promise a trouble-free life, but he does promise that he will be with us every step of the way, no matter what we face. If our lives are built on his truth, he will give us the strength to stand strong.

Step #3
Turn immediately to God.

When a storm starts to rage in your life, turn to God immediately. Our human nature is to turn to every other possible source of comfort before turning to God. We look for guidance from others; we consult self-help books; we watch Oprah; we summon our own reserves. Now, there's nothing wrong with any of those things,

112

but they shouldn't be our first stop for strength and support. Instead, when trouble comes, our reflex should be to turn to God. Remember what James 4:8 says:

Come close to God, and God will come close to you.

Next time you face a powerful storm – one that really has the potential to shake you – try asking "what?" rather than "why?" Our first response to pain is usually to demand, "Why, God? Why did you let this happen?" But the mature response is to ask, "What do you want to teach me through this, God? What are you going to do in this situation to bring glory to yourself?"

When you move from constantly asking "why" to asking "what," your entire perspective on life's problems will change. After all, you already know the answer to "why" – we live in a sinful world and bad things are going to happen. Asking "what" will help you weather and grow through the inevitable storms rather than being shaken.

> Next time you face a powerful storm – one that really has the potential to shake you – try asking "what?" rather than "why?"

The ability to ask "what" instead of "why" really comes down to the "who" in the situation. Who do you look to for strength? Again, turn immediately to God, who promises that he will give you peace if you will pray rather than worrying (Philippians 4:6-7). He will calm your fears and take away your uncertainty. When the storms come, make an intentional decision to turn immediately to him.

Step #4
Embrace the emotions.

Once you have given God top priority in the situation, embrace the emotions that you are feeling. Ask yourself, "What is really going on in my heart and mind?" God gave you your emotions; he doesn't expect you to suppress them. Look at Ecclesiastes 3:1, 4:

> For everything there is a season, a time for every activity
> under heaven. ... A time to cry and a time to laugh. A
> time to grieve and a time to dance.

God gives you the power to stand strong when things go wrong, but he also says that it is OK to cry. It's OK to grieve. You don't have to plaster on a smile and muscle through. Lean into God and then embrace your God-given emotions. He will use them to draw you closer to himself.

> So then, since we have a great High Priest who has entered
> heaven, Jesus the Son of God, let us hold firmly to what we
> believe. This High Priest of ours understands our weaknesses,
> for he faced all of the same testings we do, yet he did not sin.
> So let us come boldly to the throne of our gracious God. There
> we will receive his mercy, and we will find grace to help us
> when we need it most. (Hebrews 4:14-16)

Step #5
Lean on the faith of others.

When we are feeling worn down and depleted, we can lean on the faith of those around us for strength. To use a rudimentary analogy, think of faith like a gas tank. Sometimes – especially when we are in the midst of a storm – our gas tank runs empty. But at just the right moment, God brings other people around us who have full tanks. We can borrow from their reserve to make it to the other side.

Part of the reason God created the church is to give us a family of people who are full of faith; people willing to lift us up and give us support when we need it. A church family obviously isn't related by genetics, but rather through a common faith and commitment to Jesus. Let me encourage you: If you aren't part of a local, biblically based church, find one. You need a community of like-minded people to worship, learn and serve with – people who will rejoice with you in good times and support you in difficult times; people who can lend you their faith when you need it most. (For help finding a biblically based church, go to www.BeUnshakable.com.) When you share life with other people, your joys will be doubled and your burdens will be cut in half. Take a look at Paul's words:

> *Share each other's burdens, and in this way obey the law of Christ.* (Galatians 6:2)

Step #6
Allow your faith to be a witness to others.

As you become unshakable, not only will you grow deeper in your own relationship with God, but you will also be an example of hope to those around you. Everyone is going to be shaken from time to time. Every person you know is going to face failure, doubts, relationship problems, health issues, death and countless other storms that have the potential to shake them to the core.

So when you are able to stand strong in the face of the same types of storms that wreak havoc in their lives, they will notice – and they will want to know about your faith. Your relationship with Jesus and the ensuing strength you'll exhibit will help the other people in your life realize that they need to examine their own foundation.

Remember, unshakable faith is not about how strong you are. You and I simply don't have the ability to make it through life's toughest storms unscathed in our own strength. Unshakable faith is about how strong God is. As you build your life on the bedrock of *his* strength – by accepting and leaning hard into his son, Jesus Christ – you will be able stand through any storm that blows your way. You will be able to say, with Paul:

> *I can do everything through Christ, who gives me strength.*
> (Philippians 4:13)

Thanks to Jesus, you can face today and every day of the rest of your life with unshakable faith.

Postscript

I hope this book will become a conversation starter between us. I want to do all I can to help you live with Unshakable Faith.

For additional materials that supplement this book or to contact me directly, please visit:

www.BeUnshakable.com

You can send a FREE copy of this book to a friend at the website, as well.

And, of course, if you are in the greater Boca Raton area, please join me one Sunday at The Journey Church. I would love to meet you personally. For times and meeting locations, check out www. BocaJourney.com.

You might also want to check out our other Journey Church locations in Manhattan, Brooklyn, Queens or San Francisco.

Know you are loved,

Nelson Searcy
Lead Pastor, The Journey Church
www.BocaJourney.com

Acknowledgements

My ongoing journey in developing unshakable faith started in 1989 when I made the decision to become a Christian. But prior to that time and since, many have impacted the development of my spiritual foundation. They include, but aren't limited to: Alton and Patsy Searcy, Lela Butler, Bill and Sue Butler, Polly Branch, Ann Cannon, Doug Haulk, Bobby Gantt, David Jones, Boyce Gregory, Milton Hollifield and Rick Warren.

In addition, my lifelong friends and colleagues have stood beside me and helped me stand strong when things have gone wrong. They include: Jimmy Britt, Michel Jordan, Kerrick Thomas, Jason Hatley, Adam Bishop, Mark Rouse, Roy Mansfield, Tommy Duke and Scott Whitaker.

For major contributions to *Chapter 6 – DOUBT: Facing Doubt With Faith*, I must thank my fellow Journey pastor and previous co-author, Kerrick Thomas.

For major contributions to *Chapter 7 – DEATH: Facing the Death of People We Love With Faith*, I must thank my fellow Journey pastor, Adam Bishop.

I must also express a huge thanks to the members of The Journey Church – in all her locations – for your ongoing support and prayers. The teachings in the book were first written in community with you and first presented live before you. I love doing church with you!

My sincere appreciation to the team that has made this book and many other similar resources happen at www.ChurchLeaderInsights. com. You have no idea of the impact you are having on people around the world. Thank you Scott Whitaker, Tommy Duke, Cristina Fowler and Jimmy Britt!

Jennifer Dykes Henson has been a partner and co-creator on my last six books, and to my ongoing amazement she continues to reach new levels with each book. Her skills as a writer, editor and interpreter are hard to overstate. I cannot say thank you enough! As members at The Journey, Jennifer and her husband, Brian, serve as models of all that I discuss in this book.

Finally, I must thank the love of my life, Kelley, and my young son, Alexander. Kelley and I celebrated 16 years of marriage while I was completing this book. Kelley: I love you now more than ever! Alexander, as you continue to grow and mature, I pray that you will soon discover the unshakable faith available through Jesus Christ. Thank you both for your commitment to this book and your continual support.

Jennifer Dykes Henson: First and foremost, I must thank Jesus for teaching me to build my life on the solid foundation of his truth, moment-by-moment, day-by-day.

Thanks to Nelson for inviting me into the magnificent work that God has called him to. I am thrilled and humbled to be creating eternity-changing books with such a passionate and gifted servant.

Thank you to my mother, Sandra Dykes, for always modeling true unshakable faith in the face of life's strongest storms.

Citations

Chapter 2: FAILURE

1. Maxwell, John C. "Failing Forward." Giant Impact.com. June 2, 2010
   www.giantimpact.com/articles/read/article_failing_forward/

Chapter 3: FINANCES

2. King, Stephen. "Vassar Commencement Speech." StephenKing.com. July 6, 2010
   www.stephenking.com/news_archive/archive_2001.html

Chapter 4: MARRIAGE

3. "Kyria." August 2010. http://www.kyria.com/topics/marriagefamily/
   marriage/romancesex/strategicsex.html
4. "After Infidelity". August 2010 <http://www.afterinfidelity.com/faq.htm>.

Chapter 7: DEATH

5. Kubler-Ross, Elisabeth. *On Death and Dying.* New York: Scribner, 1969.

Conclusion:

6. Lewis, C.S. *Mere Christianity.* London: The MacMillan Company, 1960. Pp. 40-41.